CHARLES BAUDELAIRE

English verse translations © 2015 by John Tidball

First Edition 2015

Published by Bishopston Translations, Bristol, England

CHARLES BAUDELAIRE

POEMS OF 1861

Edited and translated into English verse
by John Tidball

CONTENTS

Foreword

These translations and adaptations of Baudelaire's poems are conceived as an introduction for non-francophone poetry lovers to the works of one of the most important and influential poets in the history of world literature.

From the late nineteenth century to the present day there have been many attempts to translate and adapt Baudelaire's poetry into English as well as many other languages. I hope that these new translations will convey not only the meaning, but also the rhyme, rhythm and musicality of the original poems.

Charles Baudelaire's *Les Fleurs du Mal (The Flowers of Evil)* marked an important turning point in the history of world poetry, providing a crucial link between romanticism and modernism. The first edition appeared in 1857, but almost immediately after publication Baudelaire and his editor were prosecuted and condemned for 'vulgar realism offending against public decency'. Six of the poems were banned by the court and the entire publication was withdrawn from sale.

The first edition, including the six banned pieces, contained one hundred poems. In 1861 the second edition, presented here, was published, without the banned poems but with thirty-five new ones. The complete text of 1861 is preceded here by the 'Epigraph for a Condemned Book' (which was not included at the time) and is followed by the six banned pieces. Three more poems, published in 1868 after the poet's death in 1867, complete this collection.

John Tidball. April 2015

EPIGRAPH FOR A CONDEMNED BOOK

Dear Reader, peaceful and bucolic,
With your naïve and sober look,
Throw out this misanthropic book,
This tome both lewd and melancholic.

If you've not learned your rhetoric
In Satan's school of artful thought,
Throw it away! You would grasp naught,
Or else think me a hysteric.

But if, forsaking its allure,
Your eye can fathom the abyss.
Read me, and you will love me more;

Dear curious, suffering soul, read this,
And seek your solace in my verse;
Pity me! ... or receive my curse!

THE FLOWERS OF EVIL

Dedication

To the impeccable poet
To the perfect magician of French letters
To my very dear and very revered
Master and friend
Théophile Gautier
With sentiments
Of the most profound humility
I dedicate
These sickly flowers
C.B.

TO THE READER

Stupidity, error, parsimony and vice
Consume our consciousness, and waste our body's force,
And we are wont to feed our affable remorse,
Like unwashed beggars giving sustenance to lice.

Our sins are obstinate, and our repentance faint
And when we do confess, we want a hefty fee,
And gaily we return to our debauchery,
Believing by false tears to wash away our taint.

Upon his evil pillow, Satan Trismegist
Lulls us and casts his spell on our enchanted mind,
And the rich metal of our will is thus resigned
To being vaporised by this skilled alchemist.

The Devil pulls the strings by which our deeds are
swayed,
And things that are repugnant hold us in their spell,
Each day we take a further step down into Hell,
Serenely passing through the putrid, stinking shade.

Just as an impecunious rake will bite and kiss
The old tormented breast of some senescent whore,
We steal, along the way, forbidden fruits, before
Squeezing their dried-up flesh in search of hidden bliss.

Like maggots tightly packed and swarming in our brain,
A horde of Demons feast and belch their fetid breath,
And, when we breathe, an unperceived river of Death
Flows silently through every artery and vein.

If rape, malignancy, inferno, or the blade,
Have not embroidered yet, with their designs ornate,
The banal canvas of our pitiable fate,
It is, alas! because our soul is too afraid.

But in among the jackals, panthers, apes and hounds,
The scorpions, the vultures, reptiles, snakes and all
The yelping, growling beasts that leap and creep and
crawl
Around the zoo of vice with which our life abounds,

There's one that is more hideous, more loathsome still!
He does not make grand gestures, nor shout noisily,
Yet he would gladly turn the earth into debris,
And in a yawn would swallow up the world at will;

He is Ennui! He dreams of rack and guillotine,
Smoking his hookah pipe, his eye moist with a tear.
You know him, reader, this delicate monster here,
— Duplicitous reader, — my fellow man, — my twin!

SPLEEN AND THE IDEAL

I. – BENEDICTION

When, by decree of the supreme authority,
The Poet is brought forth into this mundane sphere,
His mother, in her dread, and full of blasphemy,
Raises her fists to God, who takes pity on her:

— "I'd sooner that a nest of vipers were my spawn,
Than have to suckle this revolting pestilence;
Accursed be the night of pleasure, and the dawn
When I conceived within my womb this penitence.

Since of all women on this earth you've chosen me
To be my wretched husband's odium and shame,
And since I cannot cast this dire monstrosity
Like an unwelcome billet-doux into the flame,

I shall inflict this hatred that has taken root
Upon the instrument of your malignity,
And it shall not give forth one single fetid shoot,
So tightly shall I twist this miserable tree."

Thus does she swallow down the vile froth of her ire,
And, being ignorant of plans that are sublime,
In the depths of Gehenna starts to build the pyre
On which is consummated all maternal crime.

However, through an unseen Angel's ministry,
The outcast Child grows strong, and thrives beneath the
sun,
And everything he eats and drinks appears to be
With nectar and ambrosia blended into one.

He frolics with the wind, he talks with clouds, and keeps
Himself inspired by singing of the Pilgrim's Way,
And the kind Spirit, following his progress, weeps
To see how happily he occupies each day.

All those whom he would love observe him with unease,
Or, being emboldened by his serenity,
Compete to see who best can make him ill at ease,
And test him with their spite and animosity.

Into the bread and wine prepared for him to sup
They add a filthy mix of saliva and ash;
In their hypocrisy, they shun all he might touch,
Accusing one another of treading in his tracks.

His wife goes out in public, shouting shamelessly:
"Since he finds me so fair and worthy to adore,
I'll cast myself as some Hellenic deity,
And be adorned with gold made from the finest ore.

And I'll indulge myself with incense, nard and myrrh,
With genuflexions, tender meats and heady wine,
To see if, in a heart that loves me, I can stir
The homage due to God, obeisance divine!

And then, when I grow tired of this impious play,
My hands, dainty yet strong, will exercise their art,
And my nails, like a harpy's nails, will carve a way
Into the very confines of his foolish heart.

And like a fledgling bird that quivers in the nest,
To satisfy the hunger of my favourite hound,
I'll tear that bleeding heart, still beating, from his breast,
And cast it with disdain before him on the ground."

Upward to Heaven, where he sees a splendid throne,
Serene, the Poet lifts his arms in piety,
And the bright beacon, from his lucid spirit flown,
Obscures from him the sight of man's ferocity.

— "Praise be to you, O God, who grant us suffering,
As remedy divine for our impurity,
The best and purest essence that will surely bring
Your succour to the strong, your holy ecstasy!

I know that for the Poet you have kept a place
Among the happy ranks of holy Seraphim,
And that unto the heavenly eternal feast
Of Thrones, Dominions and Virtues summoned him.

I know that pain has a nobility unique,
That neither earth nor hell can ever undermine,
And that to fashion me a crown of pure mystique,
You must impose the laws of universe and time.

But neither the lost gems of ancient Palmyra,
Nor metals rare, nor pearls from the depths of the sea,
Assembled by your hand, can be one iota
Of this pure diadem, this crown you offer me;

For it can be made only of the purest light,
Drawn from the sacred source of Heaven's primal rays,
Of which all mortal eyes, however keen their sight,
Are but dull, tarnished mirrors that have lost their glaze!"

II. – THE ALBATROSS

Often, to pass the time, bored crewmen will ensnare
An albatross, that giant bird whose great wings sweep
In carefree indolence a passage through the air,
Behind the ship that skims the ocean's bitter deep.

No sooner have they been set down upon the boards,
Than these kings of the sky, now clumsy and forlorn,
Let their enormous wings, like useless trailing oars,
Pathetically drag beside their graceless form.

This once proud voyager has now become a freak;
Erstwhile so elegant, now mocked and travestied.
One of them, with a pipe, callously prods its beak;
Another stoops to ape the limping invalid.

The poet is akin to this prince of the clouds
Who haunts the raging storm and laughs at bows and slings;
In exile on the earth amid the baying crowds,
His impetus is hampered by his giant's wings.

III. – ELEVATION

Above the mountains, valleys, forests, lakes and meres,
Above the louring clouds, beyond the sun's bright face,
Beyond the compass of the far-flung realms of space,
Beyond the confines of the distant starry spheres,

My spirit, you go forth with great agility,
Like an athletic swimmer gliding through the sea.
You joyfully traverse the deep immensity
With an ineffable male sensuality.

Far from these fetid vapours you must soar and fly,
To seek purification in the higher air,
Imbibing, like a pure, ethereal liqueur,
The clear flame that inhabits the transparent sky.

Beyond the wearisome and all-consuming spleen
That weighs us down and clouds our lives with suffering,
Happy is he who can, upon a sturdy wing,
Take flight towards new pastures filled with light serene;

Whose lofty, noble thoughts, like skylarks on the wing,
Soar up into the sky upon a gentle breeze,
— Who hovers over life, and understands with ease
The language of the flowers and every silent thing.

IV. – CORRESPONDENCES

Nature is a temple whose living pillars speak
In words that are at once mysterious and wise,
Where hidden symbols watch us with familiar eyes
As we meander through her forests of mystique.

Like echoes in the distance that themselves confound
Into a vast, profound, tenebrous unity,
Immense as night's dark shroud and day's bright panoply,
All perfumes, tones and hues in harmony resound.

Some perfumes are as pure and cool as infants' flesh,
Sweet as the oboe's sound, as meadows green and fresh,
While others are corrupt, exotic, triumphant,

With the expansive range of all things infinite,
Like amber resin, musk, benzoin and frankincense,
That sing euphoric hymns to spirit, mind and sense.

V.

I love to contemplate those naked days of old,
When Phoebus would adorn his statues with fine gold;
When men and women, vigorous and indiscreet,
Enjoyed the fruits of love without fear or deceit,
And as the sun caressed their bodies, firm and sleek,
Took pleasure in the health of their noble physique.
And Cybele, fertile in gifts most generous,
In no way saw her progeny as onerous,
But, like a she-wolf with a bosom full of love,
Gave suckle to mankind with nectar from above.
Man, elegant, robust and strong, was proud to sing
The praises of the beauties who proclaimed him king,
Unblemished fruits, devoid of taint, free to invite,
With flesh so smooth and firm, the ardent lover's bite!

The Poet of today, when he would contemplate
Those native splendours all arrayed in natural state,
The nakedness of men, and that of women, will,
Enveloping his soul, discern a sombre chill
Before this dreadful tableau, which he truly loathes,
Of monstrous apparitions crying out for clothes!
O piteous twisted forms! ridiculous physiques!
Torsos worthy of masks! skinny, pot-bellied, weak,
That some expedient god, implacable, alas,
As infants had wrapped up in swaddling clothes of brass!
And you, women, alas! pale as a candle's hue,
Nourished and gnawed by lechery; and virgins who
Must bear the legacy of their maternal vice,
Of their fecundity paying the awful price.

We have, in our corrupted nations, it is true,
Some beauties that the ancient peoples never knew:
Sad faces, gnawed and gnarled by ulcers of the heart,
And beauty, one might say, that languor can impart;
But these inventions of our poor retarded muse

Will never cause these ailing cultures to refuse
To their most noble youth their homage to avow,
Exalted youth, of simple air and gentle brow,
Of limpid eye, as water flowing pure and clear,
Spreading throughout the earth, serene, and free of care,
Like the pure azure sky, the flowers and the birds,
Its perfume and its warmth, its music and its words.

VI. – THE BEACONS

Rubens, calm Lethe's flow, garden of lethargy,
Pillow of naked forms, strangers to carnal love,
But where life rushes in with such activity,
As wave on ocean wave, and wind on wind above;

Da Vinci, mirror dark, tenebrous and profound,
Where charming angels wear a subtle, gentle smile,
Beneath the lofty pines and glaciers that surround
The enigmatic contours of their pleasant isle;

Rembrandt, sad hospital replete with murmurings,
Adorned only by an enormous crucifix,
Where tearful prayers arise out of putrescent things,
A shaft of winter light sharply traversing it;

And Michelangelo, where we see Hercules
Intermingled with Christs, surrounded by white clouds,
With powerful phantoms rising up out of Hades,
Their outstretched talons tearing at their winding shrouds;

The boxer's angry stance, the proud faun's impudence,
You who could even see some beauty in a brute,
Great hearts swollen with pride, feeble man's penitence,
Puget, melancholic king of the dissolute;

Watteau, bright carnival where many famous hearts,
Like flaming butterflies, flit gaily here and there,
Cool decors, chandeliers, which their soft light impart
Upon the dancers swirling to some charming air;

Goya, nightmarish scenes of things unspeakable,
Of babies being boiled by witches and their ilk,
Hags with their looking-glass, nude girls, adorable,
Tempting demons, as they adjust their hose of silk;

Delacroix, lake of blood haunted by evil sprites,
Shaded by verdant pines in forests evergreen,
Where, under gloomy skies, strange fanfares fill the
heights
With music, strains of Weber, gentle and serene;

These maledictions, blasphemies and loud laments,
These ecstasies, these cries, these tears, these *Te Deum*,
Are like an echo from a thousand labyrinths;
It is, for mortal hearts, a divine opium.

It is a cry sent by a thousand sentinels,
An order broadcast by a thousand megaphones;
It is a beacon on a thousand citadels,
A hunting-horn echoing long its plaintive tones!

For truly, Lord, it is the most noble homage
That we can ever pay to human dignity:
This ardent surge that overflows from age to age,
Expiring at the edge of your eternity!

VII. – THE SICK MUSE

O my poor muse, alas! what ails you so today?
Your hollow eyes betray dark thoughts, and I discern
In your complexion both delusion and dismay,
That play upon your troubled features, each in turn.

Did the green succubus and the pink hobgoblin
Pour you both fear and love out of their brimming urns?
And did the nightmare, with an impish despot's fist,
Submerge you deep within a fabulous Minturnes?

I wish you could exhale the odour of good health
From a breast wherein dwells a veritable wealth
Of noble thoughts, and that your blood might ever flow

With rhythms, songs, and syllables from long ago,
Where, each in turn, reign Phoebus, pioneer of rhymes,
And Pan, lord of the harvest in those ancient times.

VIII. – THE VENAL MUSE

Muse of my heart, of ornate palaces so fond,
Will you, when January brings the rain and sleet,
The melancholy evenings, the slough of despond,
Still have some embers which can warm your purple feet?

Will you be able to revive your marbled skin
With the nocturnal rays that penetrate your room?
Your palate dry, your purse with not a penny in,
Will you still reap some gold out of the vaults of gloom?

You'll need, for daily bread, to earn some recompense,
As altar boys are wont, to swing the frankincense,
And sing some *Te Deum* in which you don't believe,

Or, like a starving actress, let your charms appear,
With laughter that is mingled with an unseen tear,
The boredom of the common rabble to relieve.

IX. – THE BAD MONK

Cloisters, in former times, displayed on their high walls
Scenes from the Holy Writ and the scriptures of old,
That lent an air of warmth to those exalted halls,
Which otherwise would be too austere and too cold.

In those days, when Christ's seed flourished throughout
the land,
More than one famous monk, seldom heard of today,
Would make the burial ground his artist's workshop, and
Pay homage unto Death with great simplicity.

— My soul's a vaulted tomb which I, bad cenobite,
Inhabit, as I wander in eternal night;
Nothing adorns this cloister where my spirit lies.

O good-for-nothing monk, when shall I ever find,
Within the living drama of my wretched mind,
The labour of my hands and the love of my eyes?

X. – THE ENEMY

My youth was filled with days of dark and stormy skies,
Occasionally lit by shafts of brilliant sun;
So violent were the storms, that now my garden lies
Devoid of all of its fruits of ripe vermilion.

And now that I have touched the autumn of my thoughts,
I must employ the hoe, the rake, the fork and spade,
So that the flooded land is rid of all its faults,
Where torrents gouged great holes as deep as any grave.

But who knows if the flowers I dream of, if their bud
Will find within this soil, diluted by the flood,
The mystic nourishment which they will need to thrive?

O sorrow, anguish, pain! Cruel Time devours our life,
And this dark Enemy, that gnaws at our inside,
With the blood that we lose, grows and is fortified!

XI. – ILL FORTUNE

Such a great burden to support
Would, Sisyphus, require your grit!
One's heart may well be up to it,
But Art is long and Time is short.

Far from the famous cemeteries,
Toward a lonely catacomb,
My sad heart, like a muffled drum,
Goes beating plaintive monodies.

— Many a gem lies buried still,
Far from the pick axe and the drill,
In darkness, far beneath the ground;

Many a flower gives with regret
Its sweet perfume, like a secret,
In isolation so profound.

XII. – THE FORMER LIFE

Long did I dwell beneath enormous colonnades
Upon which ocean suns cast myriad shafts of light,
And whose great pillars stood majestic in the night,
Resembling the huge columns of basaltic caves.

The billows, surging with reflections of the skies,
With echoes of a solemn, mystic harmony,
Mingled the powerful chords of their rich symphony
With colours of the sunset, mirrored in my eyes.

And there I spent my days in luxury and calm,
Beneath the azure sky, the waves, the ocean spume;
And there were naked slaves, redolent with perfume,

Who would refresh my brow with fronds of waving palm,
Whose one and only duty was to penetrate
The dolorous enigma of my languid state.

XIII. – TRAVELLING GYPSIES

The prophet tribe, those seers of incandescent eye,
Bearing their progeny, took to the road last night,
The women satisfying eager appetites
From hanging breasts, in which their ample riches lie.

The menfolk are on foot, with weaponry that gleams,
Walking beside the wagons sheltering their kin,
Their eyes scanning the skies, hoping to find therein
The inspiration to rekindle absent dreams.

The cricket, in the recess of his sandy lair,
Sees them pass by and greets them with a cheerful air,
While Cybele, who loves them, makes the landscape green,

And cleaves the desert rock to make a flowing tide
For these tired travellers, to whom is opened wide
The gateway to a future life as yet unseen.

XIV. – MAN AND THE SEA

Free man, you will eternally cherish the sea!
The sea is your mirror, you contemplate your soul
In its depths, as its never-ending billows roll,
And the tide of your thoughts flows no less bitterly.

For solace you are wont on your image to gaze,
Embracing it with eyes and arms, and your sad heart
Is oftentimes assuaged of its own aching smart
By the plaintive lament of the unfurling waves.

Both of you are discreet, shrouded in mystery:
Man, you have yet your deepest secrets to reveal;
O Sea, nobody knows the riches you conceal,
The hidden treasures that you guard so jealously!

Yet since the dawn of time you have fought bitterly,
Relentlessly and without sorrow or regret,
So strong is your desire for carnage and for death,
O unrelenting foes, brothers in enmity!

XV. – DON JUAN IN HELL

When Don Juan had descended to the subterranean seas,
And paid the ferryman the halfpenny he owed,
A swarthy mendicant, proud as Antisthenes,
Seizing both oars, made vengeful gestures as he rowed.

And through unfastened robes showing their sagging
breasts,
Women twisted and writhed beneath a livid sky,
And, like a lowing herd of sacrificial beasts,
Followed behind him with a long and plaintive cry.

A laughing Sganarelle was asking for his wage,
While Don Luis, with all the dead assembled there,
Pointed a trembling finger, with barely hidden rage,
At the audacious son who had mocked his white hair.

Elvira, chaste and gaunt, shuddered in sorrow, while,
Next to the faithless spouse who'd once her lover been,
She seemed to ask of him, for one last time, a smile
Wherein to find the warmth that her eyes once had seen.

Erect, in armour clad, a man, hewn out of stone,
Stood at the helm and cut a passage through the haze;
But the calm hero, leaning on his sword, alone,
His eyes fixed on the wake, did not avert his gaze.

XVI. – PUNISHMENT OF PRIDE

In those exalted times in which Theology
Flourished with ardent zeal and fervent energy,
An eminent scholar, one day, it has been told,
Having forced learned doctrines on both young and old,
And stirred indifferent souls to thoughts dark and
profound,
And having traversed strange and unfamiliar ground
In search of heavenly glories yet to him unknown,
To which only pure Spirits ever could have flown,
Having aspired too high, in panic and distress
Cried out, with arrogant, satanic bitterness:
"Jesus, little Jesus, I brought you great renown,
But had I wished, I could have brought you crashing
down,
Through chinks in your armour your glory brought to
shame,
And you'd be just an embryo without a name!"

And even as he spoke his reason took its leave.
The brightness of his sun was veiled in a naïve,
Chaotic cloud of doubt, and his intelligence,
Erstwhile a living temple, full of opulence,
Beneath whose vaulted naves shone such splendour and
pride,
Became a place where only darkness could reside,
A silent sepulchre to which there is no key.
From then on, like a stray dog wandering aimlessly
Across the countryside, traversing vale and hill,
Unable to tell summer's heat from winter's chill,
Dishevelled and unwashed, he looked so gaunt and grim
That laughing children took delight in mocking him.

XVII. – BEAUTY

I'm beautiful, O mortals, like a dream in stone!
My breast, where men have suffered, each one in his turn,
Inspires in the poet a love that's taciturn,
Eternal as the substance from which it is hewn.

Like a mysterious sphinx I rule the azure sky;
A heart of snow with swanlike whiteness I combine;
I shun all movement that mars purity of line,
And never do I laugh and never do I cry.

Poets, entranced by my demeanour, will revere
A bearing borrowed from the finest monuments,
And spend their days engrossed in study most austere,

For I possess, to charm those docile supplicants,
Pure mirrors that make all things fairer to their sight:
My eyes, wide eyes that radiate eternal light!

XVIII. – THE IDEAL

It never will be those false beauties of vignettes,
Those products of a worthless era's poor design,
Those feet in ankle-boots, fingers in castanets,
That will know how to satisfy a heart like mine.

I leave to Gavarni, poet of chlorosis,
His prattling herd of so-called beauties, sick and weak,
For I shall never find among those pale roses
A flower that reveals the ideal red I seek.

What's needed for this heart, profound as endless time,
Is you, Lady Macbeth, a soul potent in crime,
A dream of Aeschylus that blossoms in the south;

Or you, great Night, daughter of Michelangelo,
Who twist so peacefully into a curious show
Your beauties that were fashioned in the Titan's mouth.

XIX. – THE GIANTESS

In times when Nature's zeal was given to excess,
And every day brought forth infants of monstrous mien,
I should like to have lived with a young giantess,
Like a voluptuous cat at the feet of a queen.

I would have loved to watch her body grow in size
And flourish with her spirit in fantastic games;
And in the humid mists that hover in her eyes,
Divine if in her heart there smoulder darker flames.

About her wondrous form to wander as I please,
To clamber on the slopes of her gigantic knees,
And when, in summer's heat, she would lie down to rest,

Reclining her tired limbs in slumber calm and still,
To sleep without a care in the shade of her breast,
Like a small hamlet nestling underneath a hill.

XX. – THE MASK (ALLEGORICAL STATUE IN THE RENAISSANCE STYLE)

To Ernest Christophe, sculptor

Let's contemplate this gem of Florentine design;
In the curves of this form, so lithe and powerful,
Abound both Elegance and Strength, sisters divine.
This woman, art in stone, creative miracle,
Divinely vigorous, adorably robust,
Would grace a pontiff's couch, or merit pride of place
Upon a sumptuous bed, to charm a prince's lust.

— And see that subtle smile that lights her lovely face,
Where proud Conceit displays its noble ecstasy;
That sly, lingering look, mocking and languorous;
That charming countenance, gauze-framed so daintily,
Whose every feature says, proud and victorious:
"Indulgence beckons me and Love ennobles me!"
To such a being, favoured with such stateliness,
See what exciting charm is lent by sympathy!
Let us approach, and marvel in her loveliness.

O blasphemy of art! Fatal epiphany!
This body so divine, that promised such delight,
Is topped by a bicephalous monstrosity!

— But no! It's just a mask, a fantasy of sight,
That face illumined by an exquisite grimace;
For look: here we can see, convulsed atrociously,
The bona fide head, and the sincere, authentic face
Is turned, concealed behind the face of perfidy.
O beauty so defiled! your flowing tears awake
Such turmoil in my heart; bewildered by these lies,
My soul must drink its fill, its ardent thirst to slake,
In that great flood of Sorrow streaming from your eyes!

But wherefore does she weep? She who, so wondrous fair,
Could prostrate at her feet the conquered human race,
What enigmatic torment brings her such despair?

— She weeps, you fool, because life has gone on apace!
And she still lives today! But what gives her most pain,
What makes her body tremble to its very core
Is that, alas, tomorrow she must live again!
Tomorrow and tomorrow! Like us — for evermore!

XXI. – HYMN TO BEAUTY

Did you descend from heaven, or rise from the abyss,
O Beauty? Your demeanour, demonic yet divine,
Mingles confusedly iniquity and bliss,
Wherefore you surely may be likened unto wine.

You hold within your eye both sunset and aurora;
You spread your perfumes like an evening in the wild;
Your kisses are a philtre and your mouth an amphora,
Which make a hero flinch and embolden a child.

Are you from the black depths or from the stars of light?
Charmed Destiny pursues you like a faithful hound;
You scatter as you please both sorrow and delight,
Commanding everything and yet by nothing bound.

You trample on the dead, Beauty, while mocking them;
Among your baubles Horror reserves a special place,
And Murder, of your jewels perhaps the finest gem,
On your proud belly dances with such charming grace.

Candle, the dazzled moth flies blindly to your light,
Crackles and burns, and says: Bless this torch of my doom!
The panting lover, lying with his bride at night,
Is like a dying man caressing his own tomb.

What matter that you come from heaven or from hell,
O Beauty! dreadful, huge, naïve monstrosity!
If your eyes or your smile my spirit can propel
Into an Infinite as yet unknown to me?

From Satan or from God, who cares? Angel or Sprite,
Who cares, if you can make, — Siren or Seraphim,
Unique and glorious queen, rhythm, aroma, light! —
The world more bearable and the moments less grim?

XXII. – EXOTIC FRAGRANCE

When I, with shuttered eyes, on a warm autumn night,
Inhale the stunning fragrance of your fond embrace,
I see the blissful shores of an exotic place
Illumined by an ardent sun's unchanging light;

An isle of indolence where nature's panoply
Reveals fantastic trees, with luscious fruit weighed down;
Men that are vigorous, with bodies lithe and brown,
Women whose eyes astound with their sincerity.

Guided by your aromas to such charming climes,
I see a port with sails and masts in its confines,
Still weary from their labours in the ocean's swell,

While the soft fragrance of the verdant tamarind,
That fills my nostrils with its aromatic smell,
Drifts with the boatman's song upon the zephyr wind.

XXIII. – THE HEAD OF HAIR

O wondrous locks that frame the contours of your face!
O charming curls! O scents wafting without a care!
Ecstasy! And to fill this dark and gloomy space
With memories that sleep in this luxuriant place,
I want to shake it like a kerchief in the air!

Asia, where languor dwells, Africa's scorching heat,
Those distant worlds, whose absent wonders are so rare,
Live in the depths of this fragrant-scented retreat!
While other spirits float on sounds of music sweet,
Mine, O my love! bathes in the perfume of your hair.

I'll go where trees and men live in serenity,
Beneath an ardent sun taking their languid ease;
Thick tresses, be the swell that lifts and carries me!
Ebony sea, you hold a dazzling reverie
Of masts and sails afloat upon a zephyr breeze:

A busy haven where my spirit can inhale
A flood of sound and colour, scent and purity,
Where vessels glide on seas of amber, in full sail,
Opening wide their arms to greet the majesty
Of a pure sky where warmth resides eternally.

And I shall plunge my head in eager drunkenness
Into this black sea where the other is enclosed;
And my keen spirit, that the gentle waves caress,
Will know where you reside, o fecund idleness,
Eternal lullaby of sweet-scented repose.

Blue tresses, darkly flowing like a banner, where
I revel in the azure blue from skies afar;
Upon the downy fringes of your twisted hair
I ardently imbibe the mingled perfumes there,
The oil of coconut, the heady musk and tar.

Always! Forever! In your flowing locks entwined,
My hand will sow pearls, rubies, sapphires crystalline,
So that to my desire you never will be blind!
You are the haven of my dreams, wherein I find
The flask from which I savour your nostalgic wine.

XXIV.

I worship you as much as the stars and the sun,
O vase of my despair, O great and silent one;
I love you even more because you flee from me,
Because you seem, beauty of whom I nightly dream,
To multiply the leagues, O cruel irony,
That separate my arms from the azure supreme.

And I mount an assault, advancing to attack,
Like a chorus of worms upon on a corpse's back,
And I cherish, O beast cruel and implacable,
Even that chill which renders you more beautiful!

XXV.

You'd take into your bed the entire universe,
Lewd woman! Boredom makes your spirit so perverse.
To exercise your teeth in this singular play,
You need a new heart in your manger every day.
Your eyes, afire like a shop window full of light,
Or like a blazing yew tree on a festive night,
Abuse their borrowed power with impunity,
Oblivious to the laws that govern their beauty.

O blind and deaf machine, with cruelty aflood!
Vigorous instrument, imbiber of man's blood,
How can you not have shame, and why do they conceal,
Those mirrors where you gaze, your withering appeal?
Has not this dreadful evil that you deem so wise
Ever caused you to flinch before its very size,
When nature, so immense in its hidden design,
Makes use of you, o woman, queen of things malign,
— Of you, vile animal, — to mould a prodigy?

Contemptible grandeur! Sublime ignominy!

XXVI. – SED NON SATIATA

Bizarre goddess, whose hair is dark as darkest night,
With mingled fragrances of musk and havana,
The work of some obi, Faust of the savannah,
Ebony sorceress, child of the black midnight,

Better than constantia, opium, cote-de-nuits,
Is the balm of your lips where love's conceits parade;
When my desires toward you move in cavalcade,
Your eyes become the spring that quenches my ennui.

From those immense dark eyes, those windows of your
mind,
O demon without grace! pour me less ardent wine;
I'm not the River Styx, nine times to circle you,

And I cannot, Megaera, wanton libertine,
To weaken your defence and triumph over you,
In your infernal bed turn into Proserpine!

XXVII.

To see her undulating, opalescent dress,
You'd think, as she walks by, that she's about to dance
Like those snakes street performers show off to impress,
Adroitly waving sticks to put them in a trance.

Like endless azure skies above bleak desert sand,
Both of them unaware of suffering man's despair,
Like wave on endless wave breaking far from the land,
She goes about her life, it seems, without a care.

Her shining eyes are made of crystals pure and bright,
And in that strange, symbolic temperament that links
The inviolate angel and the fabled sphinx,

Where all is gold, and steel, and diamonds, and light,
There shines, like a vain star, for all eternity,
The sterile woman's regal, frigid majesty.

XXVIII. – THE DANCING SERPENT

My languid love, how I admire
Your form so lithe and slim,
And like a mesh of golden wire,
The shimmer of your skin!

In the deep tresses of your hair
With their pungent scent,
A fragrant-flowing ocean where
Azure waves augment,

Like a vessel that sets sail
At first light of day,
My quixotic soul sets sail
For lands far away.

Your eyes, where nothing is revealed
Of the things you feel,
Are like jewels where's annealed
Gold with icy steel.

To see the rhythm in your wake,
Beauty without a care,
You could be a dancing snake
At a roadside fair.

Beneath the weight of idleness,
Your head, my sweet infant,
Moves freely, with the suppleness
Of a young elephant.

Your body leans and stretches forth
Like a ship on the lee,
Rolling from side to side to dip
Its yardarm in the sea.

Like waters swollen by the melt
Of an icy reef,
When your mouth's nectar can be felt
Upon your opal teeth,

I taste a fine Bohemian wine,
Powerful and tart,
A liquid paradise divine
That sows stars in my heart!

XXIX. – A CARRION

Remember, O my soul, the object that we saw
One lovely tranquil summer's day:
Upon a bed of stones a corpse rotting and raw
Before us on the footpath lay.

Legs in the air, resembling a lubricious whore,
With sweating poisons overrun,
Nonchalantly displaying, with a stench of gore,
Its reeking belly to the sun.

The sun shone fiercely down on this putridity
As if to cook it thoroughly,
And so give back to Nature in its entirety
What she once fashioned lovingly.

The sky beheld the place where this fine carrion lay
As if it were a flower in bloom.
So noisome was the stench of this putrid decay
You felt you were about to swoon.

The flies buzzed busily around that putrid belly,
Out of which came black regiments
Of larvae, which flowed forth like a thick viscous jelly
Among those living excrements.

All of which undulated in a growing flood,
Or burst out with a crackling sound;
You might say that the corpse, swollen by this new blood,
Was multiplying on the ground.

And this world gave forth rhythmic music, soft and
strange
Like flowing water and the wind,
Or the grain that the peasant, working in his grange,
Shakes and rotates in his bin.

The outlines disappeared, remaining but a dream,
A sketch that reappears slowly
On a forgotten canvas, that the artist might seem
To consummate from memory.

And from behind a rock an agitated bitch
Was watching us resentfully,
Waiting to take back from the corpse the morsel which
She had let fall so carelessly.

— And yet you will one day resemble this ordure,
This horrible infection,
O bright star of my eyes, o sun of my nature,
You, my angel and my passion!

Yes! that is how you'll be, O queen of every grace,
After your last rites have been said,
When you are laid to rest in a calm, verdant place,
To rot with the bones of the dead.

And then, o my beauty! say to the putrescence
That will consume you with a kiss
That I have kept the form and the divine essence
Of my decomposed mistress!

XXX. – DE PROFUNDIS CLAMAVI

My one and only love, I beg pity of Thee,
From the deep, dark abyss in which my heart now lies,
A universe of gloom bounded by leaden skies,
Where every night is filled with dread and blasphemy;

A frigid sun hovers for six months of the year,
And for the other six lies deep obscurity
O'er land more barren than the pole's immensity;
— No beasts, no streams, no verdure in this landscape
drear!

There is no horror in the world that could outrun
The numbing cruelty of this boreal sun,
Or this dark night resembling the Chaos of old;

How I envy the lot of those beasts of the fold
That sleep without a care, to their destiny blind,
So slowly does the endless skein of time unwind!

XXXI. – THE VAMPIRE

You who, like the thrust of a knife
Entered into my plaintive heart;
You who came into my sad life
Your mad adornments to impart,

And of my subjugated soul
To make your bed and your domain;
— Vile creature whom I must extoll,
Tied like a convict to his chain,

Or like a gambler to the dice,
Or like a drunkard to his flask,
Or like a carrion to its lice
— May you be cursed, that's all I ask!

I have entreated the swift sword
To give me back my liberty;
The poisoned chalice I've implored
To banish my timidity.

Alas! The poison and the blade
Showed me disdain and said to me:
"You are not worthy to be freed
From your accursèd slavery,

Imbecile! — If from her empire
Your soul we were to liberate,
Your kisses would resuscitate
The cadaver of your vampire!"

XXXII.

One night as I lay with a dreadful Jewish whore,
Like a cadaver that a fellow corpse has sought,
I fantasized that this vile body I had bought
Belonged to one whose charms I'd chosen to ignore.

I saw in my mind's eye her native majesty,
Her candid gaze so full of energy and grace,
Her hair, a perfumed hood that framed her lovely face,
Of which my heart retains the ardent memory.

For I could fervently your noble form revere,
And from your fragrant feet to your ebony tresses,
Unleash the treasury of my ardent caresses,

If only you could shed just one effortless tear,
O queen whose cruelty your beauty so belies,
To dull the chilling gaze of your disdainful eyes.

XXXIII. – POSTHUMOUS REMORSE

My beauty dark, when you lie in eternal sleep,
Deep in a sepulchre of black marble and stone,
And when all that you have for bedchamber and home
Is but a leaking tomb within a hollow deep;

When the stone, pressing down upon your anxious breast
And on your limbs, now softened by sweet nonchalance,
Prevents your heart from beating and, stifling your will,
Stops your feet from pursuing their intrepid quest,

The tomb, companion of my never-ending dream,
(For the tomb always will understand the poet),
Throughout those endless nights that sleep cannot
redeem,

Will ask: "What does it profit you, wanton coquette,
Not to have known what causes dead men's tears to
course?"
— And worms will gnaw you as a token of remorse.

XXXIV. – THE CAT

Come, my dear cat, against my doting heart;
Take care your talons to conceal,
And let your splendid eyes to me impart
Their gaze of agate and of steel.

As my fingers nonchalantly caress
Your body's elasticity,
And when I am relieved of every stress
By your strange electricity,

I bring to mind the likeness of my wife,
Her eyes, like yours, my feline sweet,
Profound, and cold, and trenchant as a knife,

And, from her tresses to her feet,
A dangerous perfume, a subtle air
Hover about her person fair.

XXXV. – DUELLUM

Two warriors clashed in battle, and their gleaming arms
Bespattered the clear air with flashing sparks and blood.
This sport, this clattering of steel are the alarms
Of youth that's fallen prey to the first pangs of love.

The weapons are now broken, like our youth, sweet maid!
But the sharp teeth, the fingernails of cruel intent,
Will soon avenge the sword and the treacherous blade.
— O fury of mature hearts marked by love's torment.

In the ravine where lynx and panther strut their power
Our heroes have spiralled, locked in a fierce embrace,
And on the arid thorns their shredded skin will flower.

— Into this pit, this hell, our common dwelling-place,
Let's go without remorse, inhuman amazon,
To render eternal our venomous passion!

XXXVI. – THE BALCONY

Mother of memories, mistress of mistresses,
O you my every bliss, O you my every duty,
You will recall the joy of our fervent caresses,
The comfort of the hearth, the evening's tranquil beauty,
Mother of memories, mistress of mistresses!

The evenings by the fire, lit by the burning coal,
And on the balcony, veiled in a rosy hue,
The softness of your breast, the sweetness of your soul!
We said so many things that are forever true.
The evenings by the fire, lit by the burning coal!

How beautiful the sunlight on a summer's night!
How deep the vault of heaven! How strong the beating
heart!
Holding you close to me, O queen of my delight,
It seemed your very blood did its sweet scent impart.
How beautiful the sunlight on a summer's night!

The wall of darkness thickened, shutting out the light,
And in the gloom my eyes sought your eyes longingly,
And I imbibed your breath, O poisonous delight!
And in my loving hands your feet slept peacefully.
The wall of darkness thickened, shutting out the light.

The recollection of sweet moments is an art
That lets me live again those hours of happiness.
Why should I seek elsewhere than in your loving heart,
And in your gracious form, the joys of languidness?
The recollection of sweet moments is an art!

These vows, these fragrant scents, these kisses without
end,
Can they be born again from gulfs we cannot sound,
Just as the endless seas back to the heavens send
Rejuvenated suns that from their depths rebound?
— O vows! O fragrant scents! O kisses without end!

XXXVII. – THE POSSESSED

The sun has veiled itself in deep melancholy;
O Moon of my life! wrap yourself in shadow too.
Sleep or smoke as you wish; be silent as you do,
Immerse yourself deep in the abyss of Ennui;

I love you thus! However, if you wish today,
Like an eclipsed star that emerges from the dark,
To flaunt yourself where Folly goes to make its mark,
That's fine! Knife, leave your scabbard! Go your charming
way.

Let your eyes in the chandelier's light come ablaze!
Ignite desire within the eyes of old roués!
Sick or exuberant: all you are, I adore;

Be what you will, black night, red dawn or morning dew;
There is not one fibre in all my trembling core
That does not cry: *Beelzebub, I worship you!*

XXXVIII. – A PHANTOM

I. The Shadows

In the deep vaults of fathomless distress
To which Fate has already banished me;
Where not a ray of sunlight do I see;
Where, alone with the Night, sullen hostess,

I'm like an artist that God mockingly
Condemns to paint on shadows, without light;
Where, like a cook with morbid appetite,
I boil and eat my own heart secretly.

At times a spectral form in that dark place
Appears, and spreads itself before my eyes.
In its exquisite oriental grace,

When it has grown and reached its fullest size,
I recognise this visitor most fair:
It's Her! dark-hued yet radiant, standing there.

II. The Perfume

Reader, have you perchance, one day at dusk,
With gentle delectation caught a wave
Of heady incense that pervades a nave,
Or from a sachet smelt the timeless musk?

Profound, magical charm, with which the past
Transports itself into the present time!
Just as the lover in moments sublime
Plucks the fair flower of memories unsurpassed.

From the thick tresses of her supple hair,
Living sachet, the boudoir's incense urn,
Arose a fragrance wild, like forest fern,

And, impregnated with her youth so fair,
Her clothes of fine muslin and velvet were
Redolent with an aroma of fur.

III. The Frame

Just as a frame around a work of art,
Even one painted by a famous hand,
Detaches it from the surrounding land,
A strange, magical beauty to impart,

So jewels, metals, gold accoutrements
Ably accompanied her artistry;
Nothing could obfuscate her purity,
But all things served her as embellishments.

You might even have sometimes said she thought
That she was loved by all things, as she sought
To bathe her nudity indulgently

In kisses of satin, linen and crepe,
And with each movement, swift or leisurely,
Displayed the childlike grace of a young ape.

IV. The Portrait

Disease and Death reduce to ash and cinder
Our passion that burned like an ardent fire.
Of those great eyes so fervent and so tender,
Of that mouth where my heart drowned in desire,

Of those clandestine kisses that we stole,
Those passions stronger than the sun's strong rays,
What now remains? It's awful, O my soul!
Just a three-coloured sketch, a pallid haze,

Which, like me, dies and slowly fades away,
And which harsh Time, on unrelenting wing,
Erases and makes fainter every day...

Killer of Life and Art, black assassin!
You'll never erase from my memory
The one who was my joy and majesty!

XXXIX.

I give you these verses so that, if my renown
Should happily approach the shores of far-off times,
And cause to dream new human spirits with my rhymes,
Like a ship on whose sails the northern wind bears down,

The memory of you, like myths from former times,
Will bore the reader like an endless timpani,
And by a link which is mystic and brotherly
Will stay as if suspended from my haughty rhymes.

Accursed one to whom no-one but me replies
From the deepest abyss to the most distant skies!
— O you who, like a shadow's ephemeral trace,

Tread lightly underfoot, as you serenely pass,
The stupid mortals who know nothing of your grace,
Statue with eyes of jade, angel with brow of brass!

XL. – SEMPER EADEM

You asked: "When did this strange melancholy begin,
Rising like a dark billow on a gloomy sea?"
— When the grapes of our heart have all been gathered in
We know that life henceforth will bring us misery.

The pain is very simple, there's no mystery,
And, like your joy, it's very plain for all to see.
Abandon then your search, O curious beauty!
And, though your voice be gentle, let it silent be!

Be silent, foolish soul with rapture ever rife!
Infantile smiling face! Far more even than Life,
The subtle bonds of Death often around us twine.

So let my heart the heady wine of falsehood drink,
Into your lovely eyes as in a daydream sink,
And in the shadow of your lashes long recline!

XLI. – ALL OF HER

Today the Devil called on me
As in my attic room I lay,
And, seeking to befuddle me
He said: "Sir, would you tell me, pray:

Of all the things so wondrous fair
That lend her such a subtle grace,
Her azure eyes, her golden hair,
Her comely form, her lovely face,

Which is the sweetest?" - O my Soul,
You did reply to the Abhorred:
"In truth, she is a perfect whole:
Each virtue brings its own reward.

Her every feature gives delight -
What charms me most? I do not know.
She is the solace of the Night,
The radiance of Aurora's glow.

A most exquisite harmony
Pervades the union of her arts,
And no impotent scrutiny
Can separate the diverse parts.

O mystic metamorphosis
Of every sense uniquely blent!
Her breath is music's synthesis,
And her voice gives forth fragrant scent!"

XLII.

What will you say tonight, poor solitary soul,
What will you say, my heart, heart so sad hitherto,
To her who is so kind, whose beauty you extol,
Whose countenance divine kindles new life in you?

— We'll harness all our pride to sing her highest praise:
Nothing can match the grace of her authority;
Her skin bears the soft perfume of angelic rays,
And her eye clothes us in a robe of clarity.

Be it at dead of night and in deep solitude,
Or in the city street among the multitude,
Her phantom, like a torch, is on the ether blown.

Sometimes it speaks: "I'm beautiful, and I decree
That for the love of me you love Beauty alone;
Madonna, guardian Angel, Muse — I am all three."

XLIII. – THE LIVING TORCH

They walk before me, Eyes that are so full of light,
Eyes that a learned Angel doubtless magnetized;
They walk, brothers divine, bestowing on my sight
Their diamond-like flame that dances in my eyes.

Saving me from all snares and from all error grave,
They guide my timid steps along pure Beauty's way;
They are my servitors and I their humble slave,
A living torch that my whole being must obey.

Beguiling Eyes, you have the mystic clarity
Of candles burning in the light of day; the sun
Reddens, but does not quell their luminosity;

While they laud Death, you sing of a new day begun;
You sing the Resurrection of my soul and name,
Bright stars of which no sun could ever dull the flame!

XLIV. – REVERSIBILITY

Angel of gaiety, what know you of distress,
Shame, troubles, tears, remorse, vexations, lethargy,
Or those terrible nights of vague anxiety
That, like a crumpled leaf, the troubled heart compress?
Angel of gaiety, what know you of distress?

Angel of charity, what do you know of hate,
Fists clenched in darkness, eyes that weep the tears of gall,
When Vengeance beats the drum that sounds the dreadful
call,
And makes himself the prince and captain of our fate?
Angel of charity, what do you know of hate?

Angel of health, what do you know of Fever's pain,
Fever that trails along the hospice's pale walls
Like an exile that drags its limbs, and limps and crawls,
Moving its lips as it seeks the sun's rays in vain?
Angel of health, what do you know of Fever's pain?

Angel of beauty, do you know senility,
The fear of growing old, the hideous emotion
Of reading the clandestine horror of devotion
In eyes where for so long our eyes drank avidly?
Angel of beauty, do you know senility?

Angel of rapture, joy and luminosity,
The dying David surely would have asked to share
The mystic emanations of your form so fair;
But all I ask, Angel, is that you pray for me,
Angel of rapture, joy and luminosity!

XLV. – CONFESSION

Once, just once, sweet and gentle woman, did you place
Your silken arm upon my own
(From my soul's most profound and most secretive space
That memory has never flown);

'Twas late; and like a gleaming new medallion
The full moon in the heavens glowed,
And, over sleeping Paris holding dominion,
Solemn night like a river flowed.

Among the houses and beneath the porticos
The prowling cats passed furtively
With ears pricked up, or else, like the shadows of those
Most dear, walked with us silently.

Suddenly, in the midst of this intimacy
That blossomed in the pale moonlight,
From you, sonorous instrument whose gaiety
Vibrates radiantly in the night,

From you, clear, joyous, like a fanfare from afar
Resounding in the sparkling morn,
A note most plaintive, most bizarre,
Escaped, faltering and forlorn,

As if from some deformed, piteous, sickly child,
Whose kin would be so mortified
She would be hidden from a world where she's reviled,
And in a cellar cast aside.

Poor angel, thus it sang, your strange and piercing note:
"In this world lives no certainty,
And though it would an air of sympathy promote,
Man's selfishness is plain to see;

What a harsh task it is to be a woman fair,
And with what banal nonchalance
The dancing girl, with a cold and impartial air,
Must smile as if in penitence.

To build on human hearts is a most foolish thing;
All things must cede, love and beauty,
Until Oblivion consigns them to his bin
To send them to Eternity!"

I have often recalled the moon's magnificence
That such enchantment did impart,
And that horrible, whispered, secret utterance
From the confessional of the heart.

XLVI. – SPIRITUAL DAWN

When the pale scarlet dawn visits a reprobate
And meets with the Ideal that's wont his heart to gnaw,
By operation of a vengeful secret law
An angel wakes in the sleeping degenerate.

The unreachable blue of the Spiritual Skies,
For him who suffers still, though he would dream of bliss,
Opens and sinks with the strange lure of the abyss.
Therefore, Goddess most dear, Being lucid and wise,

Above the murky dross of revelry and shame
Your image, so refined in its transparency,
Before my startled eyes flutters incessantly.

The sun has rendered dark the dwindling candle's flame;
Thus, always conquering, your phantom is at one,
Resplendent Entity, with the immortal sun!

XLVII. – EVENING HARMONY

The time of year has come when on warm summer days
Each flower spreads its scent like a censer of gold;
The sounds and the perfumes in harmony enfold
The melancholic languor of the evening haze.

Each flower spreads its scent like a censer of gold;
Like an afflicted heart the trembling fiddle plays;
O melancholic languor of the evening haze!
The evening sky is like a great altar of gold.

Like an afflicted heart the trembling fiddle plays,
A tender heart that hates the black void to behold!
The evening sky is like a great altar of gold;
The sun drowns in the blood of its vermillion rays.

A tender heart, that hates the vastness to behold,
Recollects every vestige of past happy days!
The sun drowns in the blood of its vermillion rays...
Your memory shines in me like a monstrance of gold.

XLVIII. – THE FLASK

There are strong perfumes which can penetrate all mass;
It seems all things to them are porous, even glass.
On opening a coffer brought home from the East
Whose lock creaks as in protest when it is released,

Or, in a long abandoned house, a cabinet,
Dusty and black, with the dank smell of time beset,
We sometimes find an ancient bottle which might host
The living, breathing soul of a returning ghost.

Like dormant chrysalids a thousand thoughts lie there,
Quivering gently in their dark tenebrous lair,
And then, to take their flight, their azure wings unfold,
Wings that are glazed with rose and embroidered with
gold.

Intoxicating memories escape, flutter and rise
In the nebulous air; we blink, and close our eyes;
Vertigo grips the soul and sends it hurtling down
Towards an obscure gulf where human scents abound;

And it is in that dark abyss that we might meet,
Like Lazarus restored tearing his winding-sheet,
The ghostly cadaver of a rancid old flame
That rises from its slumber on hearing its name.

Therefore, when long forgotten by men, I am thrown
Into the corner of some dark cupboard, alone,
A desolate old flask, powdery, caked in dirt,
Slimy, abject, opaque, decrepit, cracked, inert,

I shall be your coffin, delightful pestilence!
The witness of your force and of your virulence,
Dear poison made by angels, whose liquescent fire
Gnaws at my heart, O life and death of my desire!

XLIX. – THE POISON

Wine knows how to embellish the most sordid room
       With a luxurious disguise,
Making the most fantastic colonnades arise
       In the gold of its crimson bloom,
Like the sun's dying rays suffusing misty skies.

Opium magnifies that which is limitless,
       Extends beyond infinity,
Amplifies time, intensifies cupidity,
       And with thrills dark and joyless
Pervades the soul beyond its full capacity.

Neither of those can equal the poison that flows
       From your eyes, your green eyes so fair,
Lakes where my soul trembles in its reflection there...
       My dreams have no repose
And to those bitter gulfs in multitudes repair.

Yet none of those can match the terrible prowess
       Of your saliva and your breath,
Which cast into oblivion my soul without redress,
       Depriving it of consciousness,
And pushing it, defenceless, to the shores of death!

L. – CHAOTIC SKY

It seems your eyes are covered by a hazy dew;
Your enigmatic eyes (are they green, grey or blue?),
Alternately tender, pensive, malevolent,
Reflect the lassitude of the pale firmament.

You bring to mind those days, warm, languid and unclear,
That make enraptured hearts shed a reluctant tear,
When, shaken by a strange and ominous unrest,
Nerves that are too alert disturb the spirit's rest.

At times you are so like those charming horizons
Lit by the hazy suns of nebulous seasons…
Lustrous rain-washed landscapes, how resplendent you
lie,
Lit by the sun's rays piercing a chaotic sky!

O dangerous woman, O fascinating climes,
Will I adore as well your blizzards and your rimes,
And in the cold, relentless winter, shall I feel
Pleasures keener than icicles, sharper than steel?

LI. – THE CAT

I

Within my fancy, on the prowl
There goes a gentle, handsome cat,
As if he were in his own flat.
I scarcely hear his soft meowl,

His tone is so discreet and warm;
But whether waking or asleep,
His voice is always rich and deep.
There lies his secret and his charm.

That voice descends most dulcetly
My soul in pleasure to immerse,
Like a rhythmic, harmonious verse,
A philtre to enrapture me.

It calms the most distressing pain,
Is worthy of the utmost praise;
When uttering its longest phrase
No words are needed to explain.

No fiddler's bow could ever bring
More consonance into my heart,
Or more concordant sounds impart
To its most vibrant, sweetest string,

Than your voice, cat of mystery,
Cat wondrous, strange and seraphic,
In whom all things are angelic,
So full of subtle harmony.

II

From his soft coat of black and white
There emanates such pleasant scent
That I was filled with sweet content
By stroking it (just once) one night.

The home is his familiar shrine,
He likes to judge, preside, inspire
All things that dwell in his empire;
Is he unworldly, or divine?

When to this cherished cat my eyes
Are drawn like magnets, then return
Within myself, I there discern,
To my most exquisite surprise

The flame, the strange, exotic rays
Of his pale, opalescent eyes,
Clear beacons, luminescent, wise,
That fixedly return my gaze.

LII. – THE BEAUTIFUL SHIP

I want to tell you, gentle enchantress, the truth
Of all the many beauties that adorn your youth!
I want to show you your beauty,
Where youthfulness is allied to maturity.

When flouncing your wide skirts with such nobility
You have the air of a fine ship that takes to sea,
Whose sails the zephyr breezes blow
Upon its rhythmic course, gentle, lazy and slow.

Upon your ample shoulders and your neck so fine,
Your head moves with the grace of a being divine;
With a most peaceful, noble air
You go upon your way, majestic child so fair.

I want to tell you, gentle enchantress, the truth
Of all the many beauties that adorn your youth!
I want to show you your beauty,
Where youthfulness is allied to maturity.

Against the silken moiré of your heaving breast,
Your comely bosom is a finely crafted chest,
Of which the panels, curved and bright
Like silver shields emblazon the reflected light;

Alluring shields, adorned with pointed rosy rings
Casket of sweet secrets, replete with wondrous things,
Of perfumes, liqueurs, spices, wine,
That fill the heart and head with transports so divine.

When flouncing your wide skirts with such nobility
You have the air of a fine ship that takes to sea,
Whose sails the zephyr breezes blow
Upon its rhythmic course, gentle, lazy and slow.

Your noble limbs, beneath the folds that they make sway,
Give torment to the dark desires on which they prey,
Like sorceresses, as they turn
The contents of a steaming potion in an urn.

Your arms, which could do sport with budding Hercules,
Could even emulate constrictors, as they squeeze
In a most obstinate caress
Your swain, as if his mark on your heart to impress.

Upon your ample shoulders and your neck so fine,
Your head moves with the grace of a being divine;
With a most peaceful, noble air
You go upon your way, majestic child so fair.

LIII. – INVITATION TO A JOURNEY

My sister, my treasure,
Imagine the pleasure
Of living in climates new!
To languidly lie,
To love and to die
In a land that resembles you!
Where humid suns rise
In chaotic skies,
Like enigmatic spheres,
Whose mystery lies
In your treacherous eyes,
Glistening through their tears.

There, all is order and beauty,
Luxury, calm and ecstasy.

Furnishings fine,
Embellished by time,
Would decorate our room;
And flowers most rare
Their fragrance would share
With amber's heady perfume;
Mirrors ornate,
And walls with the weight
Of Orient's splendour hung,
All things there would speak
In the secret mystique
Of their gentle native tongue.

There, all is order and beauty,
Luxury, calm, and ecstasy.

Galleons sleep
In anchorage deep,
Rocking gently in their berth;
It is to inspire
Your every desire
That they come from the ends of the earth.
— The sun goes down,
Setting the town,
The meadows and rivers alight
With jacinth and gold;
All that we behold
Is bathed in a warming light.

There, all is order and beauty,
Luxury, calm and ecstasy.

LIV. – THE IRREPARABLE

Can we not suffocate the old, the long Remorse,
That lives, and writhes, and would us choke,
And feeds upon us like a worm upon a corpse,
A caterpillar on an oak?
Can we not suffocate implacable Remorse?

In what elixir, in what wine, in what tisane,
Shall we drown that old combatant,
As greedy and destructive as a courtesan,
As patient as a worker ant,
In what elixir? – in what wine? – in what tisane?

Tell me, fair sorceress, oh! tell me if you know,
Tell this soul that in dire remorse
Is like a dying soldier who has been laid low
And trampled by a passing horse,
Tell him, fair sorceress, oh! tell him if you know,

That dying man who senses the wolf's patient stare
And the eyes of the carrion crow;
That poor broken soldier, how he must now despair
Of having a tomb here below!
That dying man who senses the wolf's patient stare!

Can we illuminate a dark and mournful sky?
Can this obscurity be torn
Apart, that is more dense than pitch, more black than dye,
Where there is neither evening, nor morn?
Can we illuminate a dark and mournful sky?

The Hope that that shines forth from the windows of the
Inn
Is snuffed out, gone for evermore!
There is no moon to guide them and no light within
To bring lost martyrs to its door!
The Devil has blacked out the windows of the Inn!

Entrancing sorceress, say, do you love the damned?
Do you love the untenable?
Do you know of Remorse, with poison in its hand,
To which hearts are susceptible?
Entrancing sorceress, say, do you love the damned?

The Irreparable gnaws with its accursèd bite
Our soul, pitiful monument,
And often it attacks, like some loathsome termite,
The building's very fundament.
The Irreparable gnaws with its accursèd bite!

I've sometimes seen upon a stage appear,
To the roll of a the timpani,
An enchantress who bathes a dark celestial sphere
In wondrous luminosity;
I've sometimes seen upon a stage appear

A being, made only of light, and gauze, and gold,
Bringing down Satan from his reign;
But my heart, that can never ecstasy behold,
Is a theatre where in vain
We wait to see that Being with her wings of gold!

LV. – CAUSERIE

You are a beautiful, clear, rosy autumn sky!
But sadness rises in me like a stormy sea,
Leaving, as it flows back, my lips morose and dry,
Stinging them with its salty, acrid memory.

In vain you place your hand upon my fainting breast;
The heart it seeks, my darling, is already soured,
By women's teeth and claws ferociously possessed.
Seek no longer my heart; it is by beasts devoured.

My sad heart is a palace that the mob infests,
Where they carouse, and fight, pull hair and even kill!
Sweet perfume fills the air about your naked breast...

O Beauty, cruel scourge of souls, it is your will!
With your bright eyes of fire, kindled as for a feast,
Incinerate these scraps left over by the beast!

LVI. – AUTUMN SONG

I

Soon we shall all be plunged into the frozen gloom;
Farewell, shimmering days of summers all too short,
I can already hear, like an impending doom,
The firewood crashing down on the stones of the court.

Soon my soul will be gripped by winter's icy spell,
Trembling with fear and dread, beset by storm and flood,
And, like a sun imprisoned in its polar hell,
My wretched heart will be a block of ice and blood.

I shudder as I hear each timber as it falls
With the dull sound of a rising scaffold. I am
In spirit like a building whose decaying walls
Succumb beneath the pounding of the battering ram.

That dull, relentless sound on me begins to pall,
Like the sound of a hammer on a funeral bier.
For whom? – Lately was summer; now it is the fall!
I sense that a departure must be drawing near.

II

I love the emerald light that shines in your wide eyes,
Fair beauty, but today all is bitter to me,
And nothing, not even the boudoir's sweet surprise,
Can match for me the sun reflecting on the sea.

And yet do love me, tender heart! Let your caress,
Even for an ingrate, even a wicked one,
Lover or sister, be the fleeting gentleness
Of a glorious autumn or a setting sun.

Brief task! The tomb awaits, eager and appetent,
Ah! Let me taste, my brow reposing on your knee,
Lamenting the lost days of summer's torrid scent,
The gentle golden rays of autumn's clemency!

LVII. – TO A MADONNA (EX-VOTO IN THE SPANISH STYLE)

I want to build for you, Madonna, mistress mine,
Deep in the depths of my despair, a secret shrine,
And in the very darkest corner of my heart,
Far from earthly desires and mocking eyes apart,
Carve out a niche, enamelled in both blue and gold,
In which will stand your Statue, wondrous to behold.
And with my polished verse, lattice of metal fine,
Arranged most skilfully in stars of crystal rhyme,
I shall make for your head a massive diadem,
And from my jealousy I'll cut and sew the hem,
O mortal lady mine, of a mantle designed
In stiff and heavy cloth, with deep suspicion lined,
That, like a sentry-box, shall enclose all my fears,
Embroidered not with pearls, but with my bitter tears!
Your robe shall be composed of my fervent desire,
That rises, falls, and rises, trembles, rises higher,
Pulsating at the peaks, resting in the abyss,
And covering your body with an ardent kiss.
Of my Respect I'll make you shoes of satin fine,
That surely will be humbled by your feet divine,
And keeping them within their soft embrace so warm,
Like a fine mould, will keep the imprint of their form.
If I cannot, despite my diligence and skill,
Fashion a silver moon-shaped pedestal, I will,
Instead, insert the Snake, that gnaws me deep inside,
Beneath your feet, that you may trample and deride,

Victorious Queen, redeemer of my anguished soul,
This monster swollen up with hate and bitter gall.
And you shall see my Thoughts, like Candles, all aligned
Before the Virgin's altar all with flowers entwined,
And their reflections, star-like, on the ceiling blue,
With eyes of ardent fire will always gaze on you;
And as I hold for you such cherished thoughts within,

All will be Frankincense, Amber and Benjamin,
And ceaselessly toward your snow-white peak shall soar
My troubled Spirit, seeking all that I adore.

And finally, your role as Mary to perfect,
To mix Barbarity with love and due respect,
Dark Lechery, out of the seven Deadly Sins,
Remorseful Torturer, I'll forge seven Javelins,
All razor-sharp, and then, my sorrow to expunge,
Taking your deepest love as target, I shall plunge
Each one of them in turn into your panting Heart,
Into your sobbing Heart, into your streaming Heart!

LVIII. – AFTERNOON SONG

Though your wayward eyebrows rise
With a strange and wanton air
That an angel could not share,
Sorceress with charming eyes,

I love you, frivolous one,
With a reverence divine,
Like the priest who serves the wine
In devout communion.

Scents for your luxuriant hair
Come from wood and wild alike,
And your mystic features strike
Attitudes arcane and rare.

On your flesh sweet scents alight
As if from an incense urn;
Your enchantment long will burn
In my heart, tenebrous sprite.

Ah! no elixir can wed
Ardour with your languidness,
For you know the soft caress
That resuscitates the dead!

Your fine haunches complement
Your exquisite back and breast,
And, when languidly you rest,
Cushions revel in your scent.

On occasion, to requite
Your mysterious desire,
You will lavish, full of fire,
Your caresses and your bite;

Sometimes, with your mocking smile,
Darling, you tear me apart,
Then you place upon my heart
Charms that entrance and beguile.

Under your fine drapery
And your silk shoes, I deploy
All of my delight and joy,
My genius and destiny.

With your colourful aura
You can heal my aching soul!
You can warm me, make me whole,
In my dark Siberia!

LIX. – SISINA

Imagine Diana, apparelled for the chase,
Roaming the forests, casting undergrowth aside,
Defiant, proud, breast bared, wind in her hair and face;
Her fleetness with the finest horsemen would have vied.

Or have you seen Theroigne, who loved the bloody fray,
Rousing the shoeless multitudes to take a stand,
Her cheeks and eyes ablaze as she showed them the way,
Taking by storm the royal palace, sword in hand?

So too Sisina! But this gentle warrior shows
A nature that is kind as well as bellicose;
Her courage, bolstered up by drum and musket fire,

Can also lay down arms when confronted by fears
And supplications. Her heart has, though stirred by fire,
For those who merit grace, a reservoir of tears.

LX. – FRANCISCAE MEAE LAUDES

Novis te cantabo chordis,
O novelletum quod ludis
In solitudine cordis.

Esto sertis implicata,
Ô femina delicata
Per quam solvuntur peccata!

Sicut beneficum Lethe,
Hauriam oscula de te,
Quae imbuta es magnete.

Quum vitiorum tempestas
Turbabat omnes semitas,
Apparuisti, Deitas,

Velut stella salutaris
In naufragiis amaris.....
Suspendam cor tuis aris!

Piscina plena virtutis,
Fons æternæ juventutis
Labris vocem redde mutis!

Quod erat spurcum, cremasti;
Quod rudius, exaequasti;
Quod debile, confirmasti.

In fame mea taberna
In nocte mea lucerna,
Recte me semper guberna.

Adde nunc vires viribus,
Dulce balneum suavibus
Unguentatum odoribus

Meos circa lumbos mica,
O castitatis lorica,
Aqua tincta seraphica;

Patera gemmis corusca,
Panis salsus, mollis esca,
Divinum vinum, Francisca!

IN PRAISE OF MY FRANCESCA

I shall sing to you upon new chords
O child, as you play
In the solitude of my heart.

Be adorned with garlands,
O delightful woman
By whom sins are absolved!

As from a benevolent Lethe,
I shall drink kisses from you,
Who are imbued with magnetism.

When a tempest of vices
Invaded all my paths
You appeared, Deity,

Like a star of salvation
To a disastrous shipwreck.
I shall hang my heart on your altars!

Lake full of virtue,
Fount of eternal youth,
Give back voice to my mute lips!

What was impure, you have burnt;
What was rough, you made smooth,
What was weak, you made strong.

In hunger you are my tavern,
In the night you are my lamp,
Guide me always on the right path.

Add now strength to my strength,
Sweet bath with pleasant
Odours scented!

Shine about my loins,
O belt of chastity,
Moistened with angelic water;

Bowl flashing with gemstones
Salted bread, gourmet food,
Heavenly wine, Francesca!

LXI. – TO A CREOLE LADY

In a fair-perfumed land, kissed by the sun's caress,
I met, 'neath swaying palms by zephyr breezes blown,
Where one may languish long in perfect idleness,
A creole lady blest with charms to men unknown.

Her features pale yet warm, this dark-haired enchantress
Exhibits such a noble bearing in her gait;
Tall, stately, svelte, she has the air of a huntress;
Her smiling eyes betray her calm, confident state.

Were you to go, Madame, to lands that lie afar,
To the banks of the Seine or of the verdant Loire,
Your beauty, fit to grace an ancient country seat,

Would make the eager heart of every poet beat,
Inspire in them a thousand sonnets full of joy,
And make them more your slave than any servant boy.

LXII. – MŒSTA ET ERRABUNDA

Tell me, Agatha, does not your heart sometimes fly
Away, far from the city's dark, infested sea
Towards another sea, beneath another sky,
As blue and clear and deep as pure virginity?
Tell me, Agatha, does not your heart sometimes fly?

The sea, the boundless sea, consoles our troubled mind!
What demon has bestowed upon the raucous sea,
That roars, accompanied by the discordant wind,
The faculty to soothe and calm adversity?
The sea, the boundless sea, consoles our troubled mind!

Carriage, carry me off! Vessel, take me away!
Far from here where the soil is dampened by our tears!
Is it not true that Agatha's sad heart might say
Sometimes: Far from remorse, suffering, doubts and fears,
Carriage, carry me off! Vessel, take me away?

How far away you are, sweet-scented paradise,
Where under azure skies all is but harmony,
Where everything we love must unto love suffice,
Where every heart is bathed in purest ecstasy.
How far away you are, sweet-scented paradise!

But the green paradise of sweet precocious love,
Songs, kisses, country walks, bouquets of fragrant flowers,
With violins vibrating from the hills above,
And goblets full of wine by night in leafy bowers,
— But the green paradise of sweet precocious love,

Innocent paradise, filled with clandestine charms,
Is it still farther off than China's Eastern main?
Can we recapture it, embrace it in our arms,
And with a silver voice bring it to life again,
Innocent paradise, filled with clandestine charms?

LXIII. – THE GHOST

Like an angel with savage eye
Back to your boudoir I shall fly
And to your bedside noiselessly
I'll steal in dark tranquillity;

And I shall give you, beauty dark,
Kisses that are both cold and stark
And my caresses, in the gloom,
Will be like serpents round a tomb.

When livid morning shows its face,
I shall be but an empty space
Where cold will linger till the night.

While others reign in tenderness,
I shall over your youthfulness
Preside with a regime of fright.

LXIV. – AUTUMN SONNET

They say to me, your eyes, your limpid crystal eyes:
"Tell me, strange paramour, what in me gives you joy?"
— Be kind, my child, hush now! All things my heart
annoy,
Except the primal candour nothing can disguise.

My heart will not disclose to you its secret hell,
You, whose hands are a cradle that lulls me to sleep;
Its legend, writ in flame, must its dark counsel keep;
I abhor passion, and thinking makes me unwell!

Let us love meekly, for Eros in his retreat
Secretly lies in wait to draw his deadly bow.
I know all of the arms that in his arsenal glow:

Crime, horror, lunacy! — O pallid marguerite!
Are you, like me, an autumn sky where cool winds blow,
O my so pale, so cold, so frigid Marguerite?

LXV. – SORROWS OF THE MOON

This evening the moon is dreaming lazily,
Like a sublime beauty taking her languid rest,
Who with an idle hand fondles nonchalantly,
Before she falls asleep, the contours of her breast,

Against an avalanche of satin and of silk;
Expiring, she gives way to swooning ecstasies,
And follows with her gaze those visions white as milk
That flourish in the blue upon a zephyr breeze.

When sometimes in the darkness languorous and drear,
She drops upon the earth just one clandestine tear,
A pious poet, who in sleepless study lies,

In the palm of his hand takes that tear for his own,
That tear, reflecting like an opalescent stone,
And puts it in his heart far from the bright sun's eyes.

LXVI. – CATS

When ardent lovers or austere scholars grow old,
Both are disposed to love, in their maturity,
The powerful, gentle cat, pride of the family,
Who like them loves to sit and like them shuns the cold.

Friends of both science and of sensuality,
Cats like to seek the silent horror of the dark;
As stallions of Erebus they'd have made their mark,
Had they to servitude inclined their dignity.

When they sleep, they adopt the noble attitude
Of the great sphinxes, resting in deep solitude,
Seeming to dream forever in their desert land.

From their generous loins mysterious sparks arise,
And particles of gold, like grains of finest sand,
Reflect like stars behind their enigmatic eyes.

LXVII. – THE OWLS

Beneath the shelter of the trees,
Like strange, exotic deities,
With piercing eyes, in solemn state,
The owls sit and meditate.

There, motionless, they will remain
Until the sun goes down again,
That strangely melancholic hour
When darkness shrouds the leafy bower.

Their attitude teaches the wise
To shun all movement and surprise
And to eschew life's daily race.

The man who follows every whim
Will find that life will punish him
For always wanting to change place.

LXVIII. – THE PIPE

I am an author's pipe; you'll see,
When you observe my dusky mien
Of Abyssinian or Caffrine,
That he must smoke most heavily.

When he is burdened by concern,
I smoke like an old chimney hood
In a cottage where steaming food
Awaits the harvester's return.

I entwine and surround his soul
Within the opalescent veil
That rises in a swirling trail

Of potent spices from my bowl,
To charm his heart and rid his mind
Of all the troubles it might find.

LXIX. – MUSIC

Music often transports me to the distant seas!
Toward my pale star,
Beneath a misty sky or on a balmy breeze,
I set sail afar;

Breast to the fore and lungs swollen with salted air
Like a canvas sail,
I scale the contours of the surging billows where
Night has cast its veil;

I feel vibrating in me all the emotions
Of a suffering ship;
The fair wind, the tempest and its convulsions

On the boundless deep
Lull me. Or else dead calm, like a great mirror there,
Reflecting my despair!

LXX. – SEPULCHRE

If on a dank and dismal night
A kind soul, out of charity,
Behind some ruin, out of sight,
Buries your once-vaunted body,

At the hour when the moonlight ebbs
And stars close their eyes wearily,
The spider there will spin its webs
And vipers hatch their progeny.

And every day throughout the year
Above your cursed head you will hear
The wolf's pathetic plaintive howl,

Gaunt witches chanting sorcery,
Old men sating their lechery
And villains plotting deeds most foul.

LXXI. – A FANTASTIC ENGRAVING

As its only attire, this apparition dread
Has, balancing grotesquely on his bony head,
A ghastly diadem, like something from a fair.
Without spurs, without whip, he rides a flagging mare,
A phantom just like him, apocalyptic nag,
Whose nostrils drip with foam like some convulsive hag.
The two of them press on recklessly into space,
Trampling infinity in their audacious race.
The horseman holds aloft an incandescent sword,
While his mount carelessly tramples the nameless horde,
And, like a prince inspecting his house, casts an eye
Over the cold, unbounded graveyard in which lie,
Lit by a lifeless sun's pallid translucency,
The peoples of antique and modern history.

LXXII. – THE HAPPY CORPSE

In a rich, fertile soil, where snails live at their ease,
I want to dig a deep and spacious cavity,
Where I can idly stretch my old bones as I please
And sleep, oblivious, like a shark in the sea.

I have no time for tombs or wills in wordy prose,
And rather than implore this world its tears to share,
While I still live, I would prefer to ask the crows
To feed upon my blood and strip my carcass bare.

O worms! companions dark, with neither eye nor ear,
Behold my free, contented corpse as I draw near;
Corrupt philosophers, sons of death and decay,

Feel free to take this ruin for your daily bread,
And if you know of further torments, tell me pray,
For this old soulless body, dead among the dead!

LXXIII. – THE CASK OF HATRED

Hatred is like the cask of the pale Danaïdes;
Bewildered Vengeance, with her arms so strong and red,
In vain its dark recesses from her ewer feeds
With blood and tears from all the legions of the dead,

The Fiend in its abyss has made secretive holes,
Through which escape a thousand years of sweat and
strain,
But even so, she could reanimate their souls,
And resurrect their corpse to squeeze them dry again.

Hatred is like a drunkard in a taverna
Who feels his thirst reborn with each draught of liqueur,
And reproduce itself like the Hydra of Lerna.

— But some fortunate drinkers know their conqueror,
And Hatred's retribution is to be unable
To learn the art of sleeping underneath the table.

LXXIV. – THE CRACKED BELL

It is bitter and sweet, on a long winter's night,
To sit beside the fire and hear the crackling log
That palpitates with memories of sweet delight,
And the sound of the bells that ring out in the fog.

So happy is the bell with its vigorous throat
That, despite its great age, is active and content,
Emitting faithfully its clear religious note,
Like an old soldier keeping watch inside his tent.

My soul is a cracked bell, and when in its ennui
It wants to fill the night air with its melody,
It happens sometimes that its feeble moaning can

Seem like the choking rattle of a wounded man,
Who in a pool of blood inhales his dying breath,
And struggles, motionless, beneath a mound of death.

LXXV. – SPLEEN

Pluviose, venting his ire on the community,
Pours from his urn great floods of winter's elements
On the pale inmates of the nearby cemetery
And death upon the gloomy town's inhabitants.

My cat upon the flagstones seeks to make her bed,
Shaking incessantly her body, gaunt and old,
And in the drains there roams a poet long since dead,
Whose melancholy accents tremble in the cold.

The bell sounds its lament, and the smouldering log
Joins in falsetto with the wheezing of the clock,
While in a deck of cards reeking with foul odours,

Fatal endowment of a dropsical old maid,
The handsome knave of hearts and the old queen of
spades
Discuss in eerie tones their once ardent amours.

LXXVI. – SPLEEN

I have more memories than if I'd lived a thousand years.

A bulky chest of drawers replete with souvenirs,
Love letters, poems, books, receipts, lawsuits and wills,
With heavy locks of hair wrapped up in yellowed bills,
Would shelter fewer secrets than my troubled head.
It is a pyramid, a grotto for the dead,
That holds more corpses than any communal tomb.
I am a cemetery detested by the moon,
Where like some dire remorse a veritable host
Of worms devour the flesh of those I loved the most.
I am an old boudoir, replete with faded blooms,
In which there lies a pile of outmoded costumes,
Where pale Bouchers and drawings in the pastel style
Alone inhale the odours from an open vial.

Nothing can match in length those limping, dreary days,
When, weighed down by the years of winter's icy glaze,
Ennui, the fruit of our incuriosity,
Takes on the amplitude of immortality.
— Henceforth you are no more, O living entities!
Than granite blocks surrounded by a dread unease,
Slumbering in the depths of a Saharan haze;
An ancient sphinx, unknown to these uncaring days,
Forgotten on the map, whose inscrutable gaze
Speaks only to the setting sun's declining rays.

LXXVII. – SPLEEN

I'm like a king who rules a land that's wet and cold,
Wealthy but powerless, youthful but very old,
Who scorns the flattery of his obsequious teachers,
Preferring to be bored by dogs and other creatures.
Nothing can stir him, neither hunt nor falconry,
Nor even starving serfs below his balcony.
His jester's grotesque stories told in rhyme or prose
No longer can relieve this morbid patient's woes;
His bed, adorned with fleurs-de-lys, becomes a tomb,
Even the lovely ladies of the court for whom
All princes have allure, can find no robe to don
That could evince a smile from this young skeleton.
The alchemist who makes his gold cannot invent
A method to extract the corrupt element
From him, and in those bloodbaths ancient Romans knew,
Which in their dotage powerful men do not eschew,
He could not warm the heart of this corpse dull and grey,
Where flows not blood, but water from the green Lethe.

LXXVIII. – SPLEEN

When the low, heavy sky weighs down like a great lid
Upon the plaintive heart that's prey to long ennui,
Embracing the horizon's great circular grid,
Bringing days more morose than night's obscurity;

When earth has been transformed into a dripping cell,
Where Hope, like an unseeing bat, lost and alone,
Instinctively pursues its reckless course pell-mell,
Striking its head and wings against the crumbling stone;

When the vertical lances of the falling rain
Resemble prison bars behind which our life ebbs,
And stretching wide their network deep inside our brain,
A vast army of spiders comes to spin its webs,

The bells suddenly spring to life ferociously,
Sending towards the sky their loud and fearsome sound,
Like homeless souls that rise and wander aimlessly,
Weeping and wailing as they drag themselves around.

— And a cortège of hearses, slowly, silently,
Winds its way through my soul, where vanquished Hope
is dead;
While Anguish, cruel despot, plants triumphantly
Its evil standard on my subjugated head.

LXXIX. – OBSESSION

Forests, you are cathedrals that fill me with dread;
You roar like a great organ; in my blighted soul,
Where dwell eternal grief and tremblings of the dead,
Of your *De Profundis* the mournful echoes roll.

Ocean of my despair! Your tumult and your swell
Assail me! The false laugh, the animosity
Of conquered man, his curses and his tears that well,
I hear them in the bitter laughter of the sea.

How pleasant you would be without your stars, O night!
The language that they speak is too well-known to me!
Darkness and emptiness are all I want to see!

But even emptiness and darkness, to my sight,
Are canvases where live the souls of bygone days,
Whose eyes encounter mine with their familiar gaze.

LXXX. - A TASTE FOR THE VOID

Sad spirit, erstwhile so enamoured of the fray,
Hope, whose keen spur was apt to make you run and leap,
No longer wants to mount you! Lie now down to sleep,
Old horse who trips and stumbles all along the way.

Resign yourself, my heart, and sleep your cares away.

Defeated, worn-out soul, who knew the brigand's art!
There's no more joy in love, nor pleasure in dispute;
Farewell then, sounds of brass and sighings of the flute!
O Pleasures, tempt no more this gloomy, pining heart!

Sweet Spring no longer can her fragrances impart!

And Time swallows me up and holds me in its thrall,
As the vast snows engulf a body stiff with cold;
- I look down from above, earth's roundness to behold,
But shelter there no longer beckons with its call.

Avalanche, will you carry me off in your fall?

LXXXI. – THE ALCHEMY OF SORROW

One shines upon you, burning bright,
The other brings you grief, Nature!
What says to one: dark Sepulchre!
Says to the other: Life and light!

Mystical Hermes who assists
Me, and whom I must always fear,
Of Midas you make me the peer,
That saddest of all alchemists;

I change, by your mysterious spell,
Gold into iron, heaven to hell;
And in the sky I find the shrouds

Of the dead souls I held most dear,
And in the transcendental sphere
I build great tombstones in the clouds.

LXXXII. – CONGENIAL HORROR

From this bizarre and livid sky,
Tormented like your destiny,
What thoughts to your bereft soul fly?
Free-thinking poet, answer me.

— Ceaselessly, avidly, I seek
All that's obscure and imprecise:
I shall not borrow Ovid's pique,
Chased from his Latin paradise.

O skies chaotic as the sea,
In you is mirrored all my pride;
Your vast funereal clouds provide

The hearses of my fantasy,
And you reflect the living Hell
Wherein my heart is pleased to dwell.

LXXXIII. – THE SELF-TORMENTED

I'll strike you without rage or hate,
The way a butcher strikes his block,
The way that Moses struck the rock!
And from your eyes I'll irrigate,

With waters of my cares and fears,
My dry Sahara's searing fire.
Bolstered by hope, all my desire
Will float upon your salty tears

Like a vessel that puts to sea,
And in my heart which they will fill
With drunken joy, your loud sobs will
Resound like charging cavalry!

Am I not a discordant strain
In the celestial symphony,
Thanks to voracious Irony
Who shakes me, bites me, gives me pain?

She's in my voice, that screaming elf!
It's in my blood, this black morass!
I am the evil looking-glass
Where the virago preens herself.

I am both wound and scimitar!
I am the cheek, I am the slap!
I am the body and the rack,
The victim and the torturer!

I suck my own blood avidly,
I'm one of those whom all revile,
Who is, though unable to smile,
Condemned to laugh eternally.

LXXXIV. – THE IRREMEDIABLE

I

A Being, an Idea, a Thought
That left the azure sky and fell
Into a Styx as dark as hell
That no celestial eye has sought;

An Angel, heedless voyager
Drawn by a love of hideous things,
Caught in a nightmare, beats his wings
And struggles like a spent swimmer,

His arms floundering in despair
Against the eddy's ruthless pull,
That sings like some demented fool
As it swirls in the darkness there;

Wretched victim of sorcery,
He seeks in vain to break the spell
And flee from where vile reptiles dwell,
Seeking the daylight and the key;

A blighted soul without a lamp,
Descending, in a gulf whose smell
Is redolent of a deep well,
An endless stairs with no ramp,

Where slimy monsters gawp and gape
With eyes of phosphorus that glow,
And in the pitch black darkness show
The horror of their loathsome shape;

A ship caught in a polar cell
Like some enormous crystal trap,
Seeking to find by what mishap
It came into this icy hell;

— Clear metaphors that well portray
Irreparable destiny,
And illustrate the artistry
Of Satan's work in every way!

II

A tête-à-tête both dark and clear,
A heart that is its looking-glass!
Bright well of Truth and black morass
Where palpitates a livid star,

Infernal beacon, casting wide
The flame of hell's satanic grace,
Singular glory and solace,
— Conscious Evil personified!

LXXXV. – THE CLOCK

O Clock! Sinister god, impassive, menacing,
Whose finger threatens us and tells us: *"Don't forget!*
Pulsating Torments will your trembling heart beset
And like the bowman's shaft will plant themselves therein.

Vaporous Pleasure to the horizon will flee
Just as a sylph into the wings might take her flight;
Each moment will devour a part of the delight
That each man in his lifetime is granted to see.

Three thousand and six hundred times in every hour
The Second hand is heard to whisper: *Don't forget!*
— With his insect-like voice, Now quickly says: And yet
I am the Past, I've sucked your lifeblood with my power!

Remember! Souviens-toi! Wastrel! *Esto memor!*
(My metal larynx speaks these words in every tongue.)
Minutes, fickle mortal, are gangues from which is wrung
The gold that is extracted from the precious ore!

Do not forget that avid Time has aces high
In every game! without deceit! — it is so writ.
The daylight wanes; the night augments; *remember it!*
The abyss always thirsts, the clepsydra is dry.

Shortly will sound the hour when transcendental Fate,
When Virtue most august, your still unsullied spouse,
When even Penitence (your ultimate safe house!)
When all will tell you: Die, old coward! It's too late!"

PARISIAN SCENES

LXXXVI. – LANDSCAPE

I wish, to write my eclogues in the purest verse,
To sleep close to the sky, like the astrologers,
And, as I dream, to listen to the solemn hymns
From the neighbouring belfries, borne upon the wind.
My chin cupped in my hands, there in my attic room,
I'll see the workshops, hear their banter and their tune,
The turrets, pipes and belfries, masts of the city,
And great skies that inspire dreams of eternity.

Lights in the windows, stars in the blue firmament
Across the evening haze, visions of pure content,
Rivers of smoke that rise toward the distant sky,
As the pale moon imparts its magic from on high.
I shall see spring, and summer, and autumn's golden
glow,
And when the winter comes with its relentless snow,
I shall close all the doors and shutters firm and tight
To build imaginary castles in the night.
Then shall I dream of far horizons in the blue,
Of fountains weeping tears of alabaster hue,
Of ardent kisses and of birds that daylong sing,
Of all that makes the Idyll such a childish thing.
The Riot, beating vainly at my window pane,
Will not cause me from my endeavours to refrain;
For I shall be engrossed in the voluptuous sight
Of Spring, whose pleasures I evoke with such delight,
And in the task of drawing from my heart with care
The sun that to my thoughts imparts its warming air.

LXXXVII. – THE SUN

Along the run-down streets, where shuttered windows
hide
The secret lecheries of those that dwell inside,
When the unyielding sun relentlessly beats down
Upon the fields of corn, the rooftops and the town,
I go to practice my strange swordplay on my own,
Seeking in every corner rhymes as yet unknown,
Tripping upon the words that I seek for my song,
Or stumbling upon verses dreamed of for so long.

This foster father, foe of all infirmity,
In rose and worm alike awakens poetry;
He turns our cares to vapour in the distant skies,
And fills our brains with honey from abundant hives.
He renders youthful those who walk with stick and crutch
And makes them gay of spirit and gentle of touch,
Enjoining all the crops to ripen and to nourish
The ever-beating heart that always strives to flourish.

When, like a poet, he descends into the town,
He brings nobility to things most trodden down,
And, king-like, permeates, with great simplicity,
Dwellings and hospices with luminosity.

LXXXVIII. – TO A BEGGAR-GIRL

Sallow girl with russet hair,
Tatters in the clothes you wear
Showing both your poverty
And your beauty,

To a sickly bard like me,
Your young body's frailty,
With red freckles on your arms,
Still has its charms.

You wear far more gracefully
Than a queen of fantasy
Her buskins of velvet could
Your clogs of wood.

Rather than a ragged dress,
Let a robe of great finesse
Trail its long and bustling pleats
About your feet;

And instead of threadbare hose
Where the roués' eyes repose,
Let your noble thigh parade
A golden blade;

Let your loosely fastened bows
For our sins to us disclose
Your fair breast, whose beauty vies
With your bright eyes;

May your arms invoke a prayer
To remove the clothes you wear
And may they firmly repel
Hands that rebel.

Pearls of opalescent glow,
Sonnets of master Belleau,
Offered to you by the swains
You keep in chains.

Rhymesters of the lowest art
Would to you their verse impart
When they see your slipper there
Beneath the stair.

Many a page would seek reward,
Many a Ronsard, many a lord
Would for favours gladly grovel
In your hovel!

You could take into your bed
Many an ardent noble head
And under your sway could bring
More than one King.

— Yet you are condemned to eat
Scraps of bread and tainted meat
That someone has thrown away
Near some cafe;

And you covet secretly
Some cheap piece of jewellery,
But even such scant reward
I can't afford.

Go then with no ornament,
Perfume or accoutrement,
Other than your nudity,
O my beauty!

LXXXIX. – THE SWAN

To Victor Hugo

I

Andromache, I think of you! This little stream,
This melancholy mirror, which in bygone years
Shone with the majesty of a proud widow's dream,
This pseudo Simoeis that's swollen by your tears,

Rekindled suddenly my fertile memory,
As I was crossing the new Place du Carrousel.
Old Paris is no more (the shape of a city
Changes faster, alas! than mortals can foretell);

In my mind's eye I can still see those colonnades,
The pilasters, the booths, the serried rows of shacks,
The green-stained pedestals, the tents and palisades,
And, gleaming in the windows, piles of bric-a-brac.

Once a menagerie had been erected there;
Early one morning when, beneath cold, limpid skies,
The sound of refuse workers broke the silent air
With noisy shouts and carts, there came before my eyes

A swan that had escaped from its imprisonment,
And, on the dusty flagstones dragging its webbed feet,
Was trailing its white plumage on the rough pavement.
Near to a dried-up stream the bird opened its beak,

As nervously it tried to bathe its wings in soil,
And cried out, longing for the lake where it was born:
"Water, when will you fall? Thunder, when will you roll?"
Sometimes I see that swan, strange vision so forlorn,

Its head turned skyward like the man in Ovid's verse,
Toward the cruel irony of that blue sky,
Stretching convulsively its neck in dreadful thirst,
As if it to send admonishment to God on high.

II

Paris is changing! But in my melancholy
Nothing has moved! New palaces, scaffoldings, blocks,
Old suburbs, all for me becomes an allegory,
And all my memories weigh heavier than rocks.

And when before the Louvre I pause to spend some time,
The image of that great white swan haunts me anew,
Its desperate convulsions, grotesque yet sublime,
The fruit of vain desire! And then I think of you,

Andromache, deprived of your husband's embrace,
Like a base chattel offered to a proud Pyrrhus,
Above an empty tomb inclined in solemn grace,
Hector's widow, alas! and wife of Helenus!

I call to mind a negress, phthisic, skin and bone,
Trampling through mud, her haggard eyes seeking in vain
The great coconut palms of her African home
Behind a massive, opaque wall of mist and rain;

And all those who have lost what they shall find no more,
Ever, ever again! who drink their bitter tears,
And suckle, like the she-wolf did in days of yore,
Their Sorrow, and like flowers wither with the years!

Thus in the gloomy forest of my soul's exile
Old Thoughts return, like sounds that I have heard before!
I think of mariners forgotten on some isle,
Of subjugated captives, slaves... and many more!

XC. – THE SEVEN OLD MEN

To Victor Hugo

Teeming, swarming city, city full of dreams,
Where even in broad daylight anyone might meet
A spectre! Mystery, flowing like nectar, seems
To fill the pipes and conduits of each narrow street.

One morning, in the dismal street, the sombre rank
Of houses seemed to rise taller above the gloom,
As if they stood upon a swollen river's bank,
A decor reminiscent of impending doom,

The filthy yellow fog just hung there like a pall.
Steeling my nerves as if to play a hero's part,
And arguing with my already weary soul,
I made my way to the sound of a rumbling cart.

Suddenly an old man emerged out of the mist,
In rags whose colour matched that of the sombre skies,
And whose aspect would have attracted alms and gifts,
But for the wickedness that glistened in his eyes.

Those eyes looked like they might have been immersed in
gall,
Staring as if they could sharpen the winter's chill,
And his long shaggy beard projected from his jaw,
As Judas's beard might if he were living still.

He was not bent, but broken, and his level spine
Made with his lower half a right angle so straight
And perfect, that his cane, completing the design,
Lent him the strange appearance and the clumsy gait

Of a three-legged Jew or a lame quadruped.
Onward through mud and snow this apparition went,
As if under his shoes he were crushing the dead,
And rather than detached, he seemed malevolent.

Behind him came his double: eyes, back, stick, rags, beard,
No feature to distinguish this decrepit friend,
Offspring of the same hell, and these spectres most weird
Proceeded step for step towards some unknown end.

Of what infamous plot had I become the aim,
Or what harsh chance had come to humiliate me?
For I saw seven of him, and each one looked the same:
That sinister old man was cloning rapidly!

May he who laughs aloud at my anxiety,
Who does not nurture some fraternal sympathy,
Reflect that notwithstanding their infirmity
These monsters had a semblance of eternity!

Could I have seen the eighth and yet still not succumb,
Inexorable double, fatal irony,
Appalling Phoenix, one his father, one his son?
— But I had turned my back on this vile parody.

Exasperated like a drunkard seeing double,
I went home, locked the door, gripped by anxiety,
Confused and feverish, my spirit deeply troubled
By both the mystery and the absurdity.

In vain my reason tried to keep an even keel;
The tempest thwarted all its efforts scornfully.
Like an old raft, my soul could only dance and reel,
With neither mast nor sail, upon a shoreless sea.

XCI. – THE LITTLE OLD WOMEN

To Victor Hugo

I

In any capital's sinuous maze of streets,
Where even ugly things enchant in their own way,
I watch, in deference to my fatal conceits,
As strange, decrepit beings go about their day.

These crumpled wrecks were once young women in their prime,
Eponine or Laïs! Now twisted, bent, forlorn;
But love them! for their spirit does not change with time.
In flimsy petticoats, in skirts tattered and torn,

They make their way, lashed by the north wind's cruel bite,
The clanking of the omnibus making them cower
In fright, and, like some precious relic, clutching tight
A little bag bearing a rebus or a flower.

Looking for all the world like little marionettes,
They trot along, or drag themselves like wounded beasts,
Or dance, without wishing to dance, poor silhouettes
Controlled by some vile Demon who callously feasts

Upon their frailty. They have eyes as sharp as drills,
That shine like little pools of water in the night;
Eyes like a little girl who innocently thrills
And laughs aloud at all that sparkles in the light.

— Do you know that the coffin of an ancient dame
Is often just as small as that of a small child?
All-knowing Death has made these coffins look the same,
A symbol most bizarre by which we are beguiled,

And when in teeming Paris I see one of those
Debilitated phantoms passing by, forlorn,
It seems to me that this frail being gently goes
Towards another crib in which to be reborn.

Unless, to pure geometry giving more thought,
Seeing those diverse limbs of every shape and size,
I ask myself how many times craftsmen have sought
To modify the box wherein each body lies.

— Those eyes are like deep wells filled with a million
tears,
Crucibles that are sequined by the cooling ore...
Those eyes of mystery are fascinating spheres
For those whom harsh Misfortune suckled with her lore!

II

Priestess of Vesta so in love with Frascati;
Priestess of Thalia, alas! whose very name
Only the prompter knows; vanished celebrity
Adored by Tivoli at the height of her fame,

They all beguile me; but among those frail beings
There are some who know how to sublimate their pain,
Beseeching sweet Devotion to lend them his wings:
"Great Hippogriff, carry me off to Heaven's domain!"

One, whose own country gave her grief and misery,
Another, whose own husband blighted her best years,
Or a Madonna, pierced by her own progeny,
All of them could have made a river from their tears!

III

So many have I followed, time and time again!
One of them, when the setting sun's flamboyant arc
Imbued the evening sky with its vermillion stain,
Sat pensively, alone, on a bench in a park,

To listen to the sounds of trumpets and trombones,
One of those concerts often heard in public parks,
Given by army bands, whose rich and brassy tones
Inspire heroic thoughts within the townsmen's hearts.

She sat, proud and erect, as they began to play,
Avidly savouring the grandiose parade;
Sometimes her eye would stare like an old bird of prey;
Her marbled brow seemed to be for the laurel made!

IV

Thus you all make your way, stoic, without complaints,
Across the vibrant chaos of the living town,
Mothers with bleeding hearts, both courtesans and saints,
Names once spoken by all, so great was your renown.

You who once knew such grace, you who such glory
knew,
Now recognized by no-one! An ill-mannered drunk
Makes a contemptuous comment as he passes you,
While on your heels cavorts some vile, cowardly punk.

Ashamed to be alive, shrivelled shadows that stay
Close to the walls, backs bent, advancing timidly;
And no-one greets you as you go upon your way,
Human debris who are ripe for eternity!

But I who from afar look on with tenderness,
At your faltering steps, your harsh and cruel plight,
As if I were your father, O what happiness!
Unknown to you I feel a clandestine delight:

I see your early passions coming into bloom;
I see your long-lost days, dark or imbued with light;
Your sins relieve my heart of its despairing gloom!
And in your virtues my resplendent soul glows bright!

Poor wrecks! My kindred spirits! My own family!
Each night I bid a solemn farewell to you all!
Tomorrow, antiquated Eves, where will you be,
As you meekly await your Maker's dreadful call?

XCII. – THE BLIND

Behold, my soul, they are truly a dreadful sight!
Looking like manikins; vaguely ridiculous;
Absurd somnambulists, bizarre, preposterous;
One simply cannot know where their gaze will alight.

Tenebrous eyes, from which the divine spark has fled,
Looking upwards, towards the sky, without a sound,
Seemingly ever loath to turn towards the ground
In peaceful reverie their weary, troubled head.

Thus they traverse in darkness night's infinity,
That brother of eternal silence. O city!
While we can hear your laughter and your strident cry,

Your worship of indulgence, your atrocious game,
See! I trudge onwards too! but more confused than them,
I say: What do these blind men seek there in the Sky?

XCIII. – TO A PASSER-BY

About me roared the noisy clamour of the town.
A widow, new-bereaved, tall, slender, stately, grand,
Passed by, and with a florid gesture of her hand,
Lifted and flounced the scalloped border of her gown.

Enchanted by her grace, her perfect symmetry,
Delirious, I drank, enraptured yet forlorn,
From her eyes, livid skies where hurricanes are born,
The sweetness that enthrals, the lethal ecstasy.

A lightning flash… then night! — O fugitive beauty
Whose transitory glance kindled new life in me!
Shall I see you again but in eternity?

Elsewhere, so far from here! Too late! *Never*, maybe?
For I know not your fate, nor you my destiny,
You whom I might have loved, you knew it, fleetingly!

XCIV. – THE LABOURING SKELETON

I

In the old anatomic plates
Displayed along those dusty quays,
With baubles and antiquities
And old tomes of uncertain date,

Where all the skill and all the art
Of the engraver's work appear
Which, though the subject is austere,
A certain Beauty still impart,

We see, to make the scene complete,
Like hideous automatons,
Skinless Corpses and Skeletons
Digging the earth with bony feet.

II

Out of this earth that you dig there,
Phantasmal peasants, spectral clones,
With all the effort of your bones
And of your muscles raw and bare,

What strange crop do you gather in
Like convicts from an ossuary,
And for what farmer's granary
Must you forever fill your bin?

Do you wish (emblems clear and pure
Of a too cruel destiny!)
To show that in eternity
Our promised sleep is still unsure;

That we're forsaken by the Void;
That even Death knows perfidy,
And that for all eternity
Alas! perhaps we'll be deployed

In some strange land, in searing heat,
To spend our days in heavy toil,
Digging the unforgiving soil
Beneath our naked, bleeding feet?

XCV. – EVENING TWILIGHT

Behold the charming evening, friend of villainy;
It comes like an accomplice, softly, stealthily;
The sky, like a great alcove, closes from the east,
And unforbearing man becomes a savage beast.

Sweet evening, so desired by all those who can say:
"We have, without a doubt, done honest work today!"
It is the evening that calms and brings relief
To those whose spirits are beset by pain and grief,
The conscientious sage who rests his weary head,
Or the stooped labourer relieved to find his bed.
Meanwhile repulsive demons waken from their sleep,
Reluctantly, like those who have to earn their keep,
Striking awnings and shutters in their drowsy flight.
The wind springs up to fan the street lamps' flickering
light,
As prostitution comes to life and spreads about
Like an ant colony letting its workers out,
In all directions carving out a secret track
Just as an enemy plans a surprise attack;
It taints the city's heart with its clandestine plan
Like a ravenous worm that steals the food of Man.
We hear the sounds of sizzling kitchens here and there,
The shrieking of theatres, orchestras that blare;
Cheap restaurants, where gamblers gather for their sport,
Begin to fill with harlots, swindlers and their sort,
And thieves, who never rest and know not charity,
Will soon begin their odious activity,
Quietly forcing open strongboxes and doors
To eat for a few days and buy clothes for their whores.

In this dark hour, my soul, reflect on all this sin,
And close your ears to this cacophony of din.
This is the time when sick men feel the greatest pain,

When dark Night grasps them by the throat, and they
attain
Their final destined path toward the shared abyss;
Their sighs pervade the hospitals. - No more the bliss
Of evenings spent at home, sharing a fragrant bowl
Of soup beside the fire, with a beloved soul.

But then, most of them are unable to recall
The comfort of the hearth and have not lived at all!

XCVI. – THE CARD GAME

On faded sofas ladies of advancing years,
With pale, come-hither eyes painted in lurid tones,
Flirtatious, simpering, impart from wizened ears
A jingle-jangle sound of gold and precious stones;

Visages without lips surrounding the green baize,
Bloodless, colourless lips, toothless, joyless, bereft,
Convulsive fingers groping in a feverish daze
The empty pocket or the palpitating breast;

Beneath the grimy ceilings dingy lanterns glow,
And massive chandeliers project a lurid glare
Onto the sombre brows of famous men below
Who come to squander all their sweat and lifeblood there;

Such is the lurid scene that in a dream one night
I saw before my visionary eyes unfold.
I saw myself there, in a corner out of sight,
My elbows on the table, silent, envious, cold,

Envious of the tenacious patience of these men,
And of these ageing whores the morbid gaiety,
All brazenly parading in this horrid den
The one his old honour, the other her beauty.

My heart was cowed with fear and shame for envying
These wretched creatures, rushing to the great abyss,
Who, drunk with their own blood, would prefer anything,
Pain, torment, even hell, to death and nothingness!

XCVII. – DANSE MACABRE

To Ernest Christophe

Proud, like a living being, of her noble stance,
With her bouquet of flowers, her handkerchief and gloves,
She has the easy manner and the nonchalance
Of a slender seductress flirting with her loves.

Was ever, at a ball, seen such a slender waist?
Her lavish drapery extravagantly flows
Upon her bony feet, which are daintily placed
In ornate slippers, decorated with a rose.

The frill that frames the contour of her clavicles,
Like a lascivious brooklet lapping on a rock,
Protects discreetly from unwanted ridicule
The charms that she would hide from those who seek to
mock.

Her hollow eyes are full of deep obscurity,
And her skull, set with flowers to such sublime effect,
Rocks gently to and fro on her frail vertebrae,
O charm of the unreal outlandishly bedecked.

There are some who will call you a caricature,
Lovers of flesh who are unable to admire
The nameless beauty of the human armature.
You are, great skeleton, all that I could desire!

Do you come, with your powerful grimace, to upset
The festival of Life? Or does some ancient fire,
Still burning in your living carcass, spur you yet
To credulously seek the Sabbath of Desire?

Do you hope that the violin's sweet melody,
Or the candle's bright flame, will banish your unrest,
And do you come to ask the flood of revelry
To quench the flames of hell that burn within your breast?

Inexhaustible well of folly and of sin!
Endless distillery of ancient suffering!
Through the curved trellis of your ribs, I see therein
The insatiable viper ever wandering.

Indeed to tell the truth, I fear your coquetry,
Despite its diligence, will not find just reward;
What mortal heart could understand your raillery?
Only to strong men does horror its charms accord!

Inducing vertigo, the abyss of your eyes
Exhales dire thoughts, and prudent dancers will revile,
With floods of bitter gall that in their souls arise,
The two-and-thirty teeth of your eternal smile.

But who's not held a skeleton in his embrace,
And who on sombre thoughts of tombs has never fed?
What matter fragrances, fine clothes of silk and lace?
Those who think they are handsome often scorn the dead.

Bayadere with no nose, inexorable *gouge*,
Tell all these dancers who pretend to take offence:
"Proud dears, despite the art of powder and of rouge,
All of you smell of death! Skeletons filled with scents

Of musk, shrivelled Antinoüs, bald-pated beaux,
Varnished cadavers, old lovelaces with white hair,
This dance of death, this universal fandango
Leads you to places that you never knew were there!

From the Seine's icy banks to Ganges' baking ground,
The herd of mortal men cavorts, oblivious
To the approach of the dark Angel's trumpet sound
That threatens in the sky like a dark blunderbuss.

In all climes, under every sun, all-seeing Death
Admires your antics, risible Humanity,
And often, just like you, with perfume on her breath,
Mingles her irony with your insanity!"

XCVIII. – THE LOVE OF FALSEHOOD

When I see you, as on your languid way you go,
To the soft echo of a plaintive melody,
Suspending your demeanour, elegant and slow,
And showing in your gaze the depth of your ennui;

When I behold, lit by the gas-lamp's ghostly light,
Your pallid brow, embellished by a morbid trait,
Illumined, like a dawn, by lanterns of the night,
And your alluring eyes like those of a portrait,

I tell myself: how fair she is! how strangely fresh!
The towering memories, that crown her from above,
So regally; her heart, bruised like a ripened peach,
Is ready, like her body, for a knowing love.

Are you autumnal fruit, whose flavour is supreme?
A funeral urn awaiting tears in solemn hours,
A perfume that of far oases brings a dream,
Caressing pillow, or a basket full of flowers?

I know that there are eyes, always melancholic,
That have no precious secrets, do not harbour lies;
Caskets without jewels, lockets without relics,
More empty, more profound than even you, O Skies!

But does it not suffice that you are just a semblance
That brings joy to a heart fleeing from truth and duty?
What matter your folly, or your indifference?
Mask or adornment - hail! I worship your beauty.

XCIX.

I shall never forget our little cottage there,
Close to the town, but blessed with a most tranquil air;
A plaster Pomona and an old Aphrodite,
Stood in a little copse, to hide their nudity;
And the bright evening sun, whose slanting rays of gold
Behind the window pane were wondrous to behold,
Appeared to contemplate with a curious eye
Our silent evening meal from its home in the sky,
And like a candle's glow its mellow radiance cast
On the old tablecloth and our frugal repast.

C.

The servant with a heart of gold who sleeps alone,
Far from your jealous gaze, beneath a humble stone,
Should we not take her just a little bunch of flowers?
The dead, the wretched dead, endure such sombre hours,
And when the melancholy wind of autumn blows
Around the marble slabs beneath which they repose,
The living must seem so ungrateful to the dead,
As they lie sleeping snug and cosy in their bed,
While they, the dead, gnawed by a sombre reverie,
Without a bedfellow to keep them company,
Frozen old skeletons upon whom worms have fed,
They feel the winter snows drip on their stony bed,
The passing of the years, with neither family
Nor friend to tend their grave in the bleak cemetery.

If I saw her one evening, calmly sitting there
Beside the whistling fire logs, in her rocking chair;
If, in the cheerless twilight of December's gloom
I found her crouching in a corner of my room,
Forsaking the cold churchyard where she used to lie
To watch over her child with a maternal eye,
What would I find to say, after so many years,
To this devoted soul who sheds such loving tears?

CI. – MIST AND RAIN

O late autumnal days, winter and mud-soaked spring,
O dormant seasons, how I praise the joy you bring!
For you surround my heart and envelop my brain
In a vaporous shroud, a tomb of mist and rain.

In this vast plain where the cold winds of winter course,
Where in long drawn-out nights the weathercock grows
hoarse,
My spirit, more at ease with what the winter brings
Than with renascent springtime, opens wide its wings.

Nothing could be more sweet to a heart filed with doom,
So long acquainted with the hoarfrosts and the rimes,
O colourless seasons, pale monarchs of our climes,

Than the eternal aspect of your pallid gloom,
— Except perhaps, one moonless evening, head to head,
To send our woes to sleep on an intrepid bed.

CII. – A PARISIAN DREAM

I

Of that most awe-inspiring scene,
Such as mere mortals never see,
That lay before me in a dream,
The image still enraptures me.

Indeed sleep is a wondrous thing!
And by a singular caprice
I had excluded anything
That grows at random from the piece;

And, proud of my fine artistry,
I savoured in this rare tableau
The breathtaking monotony
Of metal, stone, and water-flow.

Babel of stairways and arcades
And endless palaces unrolled,
With limpid pools and great cascades
Falling on matte and burnished gold.

And even greater waterfalls,
Like crystal curtains hanging there,
Cascaded down metallic walls
As if suspended in the air.

The dormant pools, instead of trees
Were circumscribed by colonnades,
Where giant naiads took their ease,
Admiring their reflected gaze.

Lakes of blue water outward flowed
Between the rose and emerald quays,
Like an endless aquatic road,
To the earth's furthest boundaries.

Magical waves, embellished by
Exquisite gemstones that adorned

Enormous mirrors, dazzled by
The radiance of reflected forms.

Insouciant and taciturn,
Ganges flowed in the firmament,
Pouring rich treasures from its urn
Into great gulfs of diamond.

Architect of my fantasy,
I made, out of a quiet rill,
To flow within an artery
An ocean I could tame at will;

And all the colours, even black,
Seemed iridescent, burnished bright;
The liquid gave its splendour back
In crystal rays of purest light.

No moon, no stars, nor any sign
Of sunlight to give luminance
To this prodigious scene of mine,
That shone with its own radiance.

And on this wondrous vision here
There hovered (awful novelty!
All for the eyes, naught for the ear!)
A silence of eternity.

II

I opened my bewildered eyes
And saw again the wretched hole
Wherein I dwelt, and felt arise
The pangs of anguish in my soul;

The doleful pendulum struck noon,
In accents brutal and perverse,
And from the sky a dreadful gloom
Pervaded the dull universe.

CIII. – MORNING TWILIGHT

Across the barracks yard the loud reveille came,
And the strong morning breeze disturbed the lantern's
flame.

It was the hour when swarthy adolescent boys
Lie dreaming on their pillows of forbidden joys;
When, like a blood-shot eye that palpitates with dread,
The lantern on the daylight makes a patch of red;
And when the soul, weighed down by sombre disarray,
Mimics the combat of the lantern and the day.
Like weeping eyes upon whose tears the breezes play,
The trembling air pulsates with all that flees away,
Men grow weary of writing, women of lovers' play.

Chimneys began to smoke as night gave way to day.
Women of pleasure, eyelids painted vulgarly,
Were sleeping open-mouthed in stupid reverie,
While others, destitute, their bosoms cold and blue,
Breathed on the dying embers, and on their fingers too.
It was the hour when, due to cold and penury,
Women in childbirth are more prone to agony;
And like a sob that's choked by frothy blood and gall,
A distant rooster pierced the dank air with its call;
A sea of fog enveloped windows, doors and walls,
And those who agonised inside the hospitals
Uttered the final rattles of their wretched lives.
The weary debauchees returned home to their wives.

Aurora, shivering in robe of rose and green,
Slowly advanced along the still deserted Seine,
And sombre Paris rubbed his eyes as day began,
And gathered up his tools, industrious old man.

WINE

CIV. – THE SOUL OF THE WINE

One night the soul of wine was singing in the flasks:
"O Man, I send to you, in your most wretched state,
From my glass prison, sealed by the vermilion wax,
A poem full of light and brotherly estate.

I know how much devotion, how much sweat and toil,
Upon the burning hill, beneath a leaden sun,
Is needed to engender in me life and soul;
But I am not ungrateful, when all's said and done.

For I am filled with joy when gladly I succumb
Upon the eager throat of one consumed by toil,
Whose warm oesophagus provides a pleasant tomb
Where I am more content than in the cellar's chill.

Do you not hear the hope that beats within my heart?
The sound of merriment in Sunday's happy song?
Sleeves rolled and glasses raised you'll celebrate my art
And glorify my name in verses loud and long.

I shall inspire delight in your dear lady's eyes,
Restore unto your son his colour and aplomb,
And that frail athlete of this life will surely prize
This oil that firms the flesh and makes the muscles strong.

In you I shall descend, ambrosia of the earth,
A precious seed that's sown by the eternal sower,
So that out of our love a poem shall have birth,
Ascending heavenward to God like a rare flower."

CV. – THE RAG-PICKERS' WINE

Often, beneath a street-lamp's flickering red flame,
As the night wind springs up, rattling the glassy frame,
In the old quarter's muddy, labyrinthine maze,
Where in a seething ferment crawls the human race,

One comes upon a ragman, nodding busily,
Stumbling and bumping into pillars, carelessly,
And paying no attention to disloyal sneaks,
He pours his heart out in the plans of which he speaks.

He swears a solemn oath, proclaiming laws sublime,
Roundly denouncing crooks, backing victims of crime,
And underneath the sky's suspended canopy
Grows drunken with his virtue and integrity.

Yes, these folk burdened by the chores of daily life,
Worn out by age and tormented by toil and strife,
Weighed down by all their woes, beset by fear and doubt,
Crushed by the piles of dross that Paris vomits out,

Return, redolent with the odour of the cask,
With their comrades-in-arms, pale from their daily task,
Whose whiskers droop like faded pennants as they march.
Banners, standards and flowers, and a triumphal arch

Rise up before their eyes, in solemn majesty!
And in the deafening and luminous orgy
Of trumpets, shouting, drums, and blazing sun above,
They bring a taste of glory to a people drunk with love!

And thus it is that wine, like Pactolus of old,
Throughout Humanity frivolously rolls its gold,
And in men's throats of its great deeds is wont to sing,
And by dint of its prowess reigns just like a king.

To drown their bitter thoughts and calm antipathy
In all those blighted souls who die in misery,
God, in remorse, invented sleep for everyone;
And then Man added Wine, sacred child of the Sun!

CVI. – THE ASSASSIN'S WINE

My wife is dead, and I am free!
So now I can drink all I like.
When I came home without a mite,
Her wailing used to torture me.

I am as happy as a king;
The air is pure, the sky is blue,
Just like that summer when I knew
That a romance was blossoming!

This awful thirst that grows apace
Would need, to quench it, truth be told,
As much wine as her tomb could hold;
And that's a pretty roomy place:

I threw her body down a well,
I even pushed on top of it
As many stones as I could fit.
— Will I forget her? Time will tell!

By virtue of our solemn oath
That nothing ever can defile,
And so that we might reconcile
Ourselves, as when we pledged our troth,

I asked to meet her once again,
One night in a secluded place.
She came - mad creature! (grant her grace!).
We are all more or less insane!

She was still such a pretty wife,
Though rather tired and worn! And I
Loved her too much! And that is why
I said to her: Depart this life!

No-one can understand my mind.
Did any sot, addled by drink,
In his most morbid fancy think
To make a winding-sheet of wine?

That unshakable philistine,
Impervious as a steel machine,
Even in his most ardent dream,
Love's raptures never could divine,

With its enchantments and its pains,
Its winding trail of doubts and fears,
Its poisoned chalices, its tears,
Its sounds of rattling bones and chains.

— So here I am, free and alone!
Tonight I'll be blind drunk, of course;
And then without fear or remorse,
I shall lie down on the cold stone,

And there I'll sleep, out like a light!
The heavy wheels of a huge truck,
Loaded with earth and stones and muck,
Careering down the highway, might

As well shatter my guilty head
Or slice my body clean in two,
I've had enough of all of you:
God, Satan and the Holy Bread!

CVII. – THE LONELY MAN'S WINE

A handsome courtesan's intoxicating gaze,
That glides towards us like the pale transparent beam
The undulating moon sends to the trembling stream,
Where carelessly she bathes the beauty of her rays;

The final bag of florins that a gambler holds;
Or a wanton embrace from slender Annaliese;
The gentle yet unnerving sounds of melodies,
Resembling distant cries of sorrows unconsoled;

None of these things, O bottle wide and deep, is worth
The penetrating balm that your abundant girth
Reserves for the devoted poet's thirsting heart;

You give him youth and hope, those enemies of doubt,
— And pride, that priceless treasure of the down-and-out,
That gives us grandeur and, like Gods, sets us apart!

CVIII. – THE LOVERS' WINE

How splendid is the world today!
Without bit or spur, lets away
Upon our mounts of heady wine
To heavens magic and divine!

Like two angels tormented by
An ardent flame that will not die,
In the bright morning's crystal blue
Let us our distant dream pursue.

Riding and rocking languidly
On an all-knowing, swirling tide,
In a parallel ecstasy,

My sister, floating side by side,
We'll follow these exotic streams
To the paradise of my dreams!

FLOWERS OF EVIL

CIX. – DESTRUCTION

Forever on my back, the Devil does not rest;
He hovers over me with his mysterious fire;
I breathe him in and feel the flame within my breast,
Filling me with relentless, culpable desire.

Sometimes, knowing my love of Art, he takes the shape
Of a woman, seductive, proud, promiscuous,
And under specious pretexts that I can't escape,
Acquaints my eager lips with philtres infamous.

He leads me thus, far from the watchful eye of God,
Panting, and broken with fatigue, on paths untrod,
Amid the plains of Ennui, fearful and alone,

And casts before my horrified, bewildered eyes
Filthy apparel, gaping wounds of blood and bone,
And all of foul Destruction's macabre supplies.

CX. – A MARTYR (DRAWING BY AN UNKNOWN MASTER)

Amid the perfume flasks and fabrics of lamé,
The furniture of jet and gold,
The marbles, paintings, and the fine-scented array
Proudly trailing its sumptuous folds,

In a sultry boudoir, redolent of decay
And the oppressive stench of death,
Where, in its glass coffin, a withering bouquet
Exhales its final dying breath,

A headless corpse pours out, in a cascade that bursts
Onto the covers of the bed,
A tide of blood on which the fabric slakes its thirst,
A living stream of vibrant red.

Like those pale visions that entrap our curious stare,
Visions born of obscurity,
The head, with its thick mass of dark, luxuriant hair
And its expensive jewellery,

Upon a small commode, like a ranunculus,
Is resting. From unseeing eyes
A vague, bewildered look, both pale and tenebrous,
Expresses horror and surprise.

The naked torso, on the bed, lies motionless,
Displaying, by a lantern lit,
The secret splendour and the fatal comeliness
That nature had bestowed on it;

A rose-hued stocking, flecked with gold, adorns the thigh,
Like a macabre souvenir;
The garter, glistening like a secretive eye,
Emits a diamantine leer.

The singular aspect of all this solitude,
And the portrait that hangs above

With its strange eyes and its alluring attitude,
Tokens of a tenebrous love,

Reveal clandestine joys and esoteric rites,
Demonic lecheries untold,
Of which malignant angels savoured the delights,
Hovering in the curtains' folds;

And yet, to judge by the elegant shapeliness
Of the exquisite shoulder's rake,
The slightly pointed haunches, the waist's slenderness,
Suggestive of a writhing snake,

She is still young! - Did her exasperated soul
And her senses, gnawed by ennui,
Give way to wandering desires, losing control
In frenzies of debauchery?

Vindictive man whose lust, living, you could not sate
Despite much love, nor quench his fire,
Did he upon your yielding body consummate
The magnitude of his desire?

Reply, impure cadaver! and did he, by your hair,
Lift you up with a fevered fist,
O gruesome head, tell me: did he, holding you there,
Plant on your teeth his farewell kiss?

— Far from the sneering world, far from the tainted mob,
Far from the harbingers of doom,
Sleep peacefully, sleep well, bizarre creature of God,
In the peace of your secret tomb;

Your spouse may roam the world, but your immortal
wraith
Watches his every sleeping breath;
No doubt, as you do, he will likewise keep the faith,
And remain constant until death.

CXI. – DAMNED WOMEN

Like pensive beasts, they lie motionless on the sands,
Scanning the skyline of the oceans with their eyes,
And, feet caressing feet, and hands entwined in hands,
Temper the pain of love with gentle languid sighs.

Some, whose hearts are immersed in the language of love,
Deep in secluded groves where brooks chatter and tease,
Spelling out childish promises of constant love,
Inscribed upon the bark of burgeoning young trees;

Others, like nuns, walk slowly, gravely and in fear,
Across the rocky paths beneath the mountain crests,
Where Saint Anthony first in visions saw appear,
To tempt his mortal soul, the naked, rose-hued breasts.

Some there are who, lit by a resin lamp's dull flame,
Deep in the silent hollow of some pagan place,
To calm their wretched fevers loudly call your name,
O Bacchus, sleep-inducing healer of malaise!

And others, with a liking for monastic dress,
Who, with a whip concealed in their accoutrement,
Mingle, in sombre woods and nights of loneliness,
The froth of pleasure with the tears of their torment.

O virgins, O demons, O monsters, O martyrs,
Immense spirits disdainful of reality,
Seeking infinity, believers and satyrs,
Now uttering loud cries, now weeping bitterly.

Poor sisters, whom my soul has followed in your hell,
I love you and I pity you in equal parts,
For all your dark despair, your thirsts life cannot quell,
And the great urns of love that fill your bounteous hearts!

CXII. – THE TWO GOOD SISTERS

Debauchery and Death are two lovable twins,
Lavish with the delights and pleasures of this earth,
Whose rag-clad virgin loins, unsullied by their sins,
Toiling eternally, have never given birth.

For the sinister poet, foe of families,
Favoured by the abyss, sycophant on low pay,
Both sepulchres and brothels, in their sanctuaries,
Have beds in which remorse and penance never lay.

Both coffin and alcove, so rich in blasphemy,
Offer us each in turn, like sisters good and true
Sweet lusts and dreadful pleasures to charm us anew.

When will you bury me, sublime Debauchery?
O Death, who rival her allure, when will it be
That you graft your dark cypress on her myrtle tree?

CXIII. – THE FOUNTAIN OF BLOOD

Sometimes it seems to me my blood is flowing free,
Bubbling as from a fountain, sobbing rhythmically.
It flows like swollen rivers after heavy rain,
But the wound whence it flows is always sought in vain.

Across the city streets it flows mile upon mile,
Transforming every paving stone into an isle,
Creating food by which every creature is fed,
And colouring all nature with flamboyant red.

I've often asked deceiving wines to find a way
To dull the pain I feel, if only for a night!
But wine sharpens the senses and improves the sight!

I've sought in carnal love my torments to allay;
But love for me is but a painful bed of thorns,
Made to provide the food and drink of cruel whores!

CXIV. – ALLEGORY

Picture a woman, beautiful and sleek of line,
Her locks of auburn hair trailing in scarlet wine,
Talons of love, sweet poisons of those dens of sin,
Slide over and are blunted on her granite skin.
She treats Death with disdain and flaunts Debauchery,
Those two monsters whose hands are working constantly
At their destructive games, yet have shown fealty
To her exquisite body's untamed majesty.
A goddess when she walks, a sultana at leisure,
She shows a heathen's faith in her pursuit of pleasure;
Her eyes, her ample breasts, and her wide open arms
Invite the human race to celebrate her charms.
She thinks, indeed she knows, that she cannot give birth,
And yet she is so vital to this complex earth;
She knows that woman's beauty is a gift sublime
That warrants absolution from all shameful crime.
She knows nothing of Hell, nor yet of Purgatory,
And when the time is come to face eternity
She'll look Death in the face, and she'll accept her fate
Just like a new-born child, — without remorse or hate.

CXV. – THE BEATRICE

As through a barren land I wandered aimlessly,
Berating nature and complaining bitterly,
Sharpening slowly on the whetstone of my heart
The knife with which my thoughts were tearing me apart,
I saw, in the full noon, descending on my head,
A huge macabre cloud that filled my soul with dread,
For therein I beheld a veritable herd
Of dwarf-like demons, cruel, curious, absurd.
Sullenly they began to look me up and down,
And, just as passers-by might stop to watch a clown,
I heard them sniggering and talking quietly,
Exchanging gestures as they contemplated me:

— "Let's take a while to contemplate this travesty,
Who Hamlet's tragic posture seeks to parody,
With indecisive look and long, dishevelled hair.
Is it not pitiful to see the anxious stare
Of this penniless hack trying to play a part?
For he's convinced that he is practised in his art,
Seeking to interest in his dull tales of woe
The eagles, crickets, flowers, even the streams that flow,
And even we, the authors of these old conceits,
Must hear the long tirades he shouts about the streets!"

I could (being the lord and master of my pride,
Impervious to the insults that they multiplied)
Have simply turned my back abruptly, and ignored
Their jibes, had I not seen among that loathsome horde,
(O crime that might have caused even the sun to move!)
The queen of my desire, my one and only love,
Laughing aloud with them and mocking my distress,
And even sharing with them an obscene caress.

CXVI. – A VOYAGE TO CYTHERA

My heart, just like a bird, was winging joyfully,
Hovering free about the rigging, soaring high;
The ship serenely sailed beneath a cloudless sky,
Majestic in the sun's resplendent panoply.

What is this gloomy isle, this sombre port of call?
— It's Cythera, we're told, a land famous in song,
Banal utopia for which old roués long.
But look, it's just a dismal country after all.

— Island of secrets and indulgence of the heart!
The proud spirit of Venus hovers fragrantly
Above your fabled seas, as in antiquity,
Upon enchanted souls love's languor to impart.

Fair isle of myrtles green, and flowers that unclose
Their charms to every nation's venerating eyes,
Where of adoring hearts the everlasting sighs
Imbue with frankincense gardens of blue and rose

Or mingle sweetly with a dove's eternal moan!
— Cythera had become a dark and barren land,
A wretched crow-infested place of rock and sand.
However, I discerned something that stood alone!

It was no ancient temple shaded by tall trees,
Where a young priestess, lover of exotic flowers,
Obsessed by secret dreams, might while away the hours,
Her silken robe half opened by the passing breeze;

But as we hugged the coast, as close as we could get,
The birds scattered, and we could only stand and stare:
Before our startled gaze a three-armed gibbet there
Stood out against the sky in sombre silhouette.

Ferocious birds were perched upon their carrion prey,
A rotting corpse that must have hung there for a week,
Each planting the sharp point of its repulsive beak
In every bloody corner of that foul decay.

The eyes were just two holes, and from the open loin
The intestines spilled out and fell onto the thighs,
And his torturers had, O hideous surprise!
Ripped out the very manhood from his gaping groin.

Beneath the feet, a herd of jealous quadrupeds
Circled impatiently, sniffing the putrid air;
And a much larger beast, prowling amongst them there,
Seemed like an executioner among his aides.

Native of Cythera, child of its bounteous womb,
You suffered silently and paid an awful price
In expiation for your infamy and vice,
And all the sins that have deprived you of a tomb.

Ridiculous hanged man, I share all of your pain!
And seeing your limbs hanging there, I must confess
I felt the nausea ascending in my breast,
The gall of former sorrows rising once again;

Poor devil, you stirred in me memories afresh;
I could feel every beak and every gnashing tooth
Of those rapacious crows and panthers of my youth
Who once took such delight in savouring my flesh.

— The sky was azure blue, and calm suffused the sea;
For me the sky was hidden by a sombre cloud,
Alas! and as if wrapped in a funereal shroud,
My heart was buried deep inside this allegory.

O Venus, I found nothing on your island! Just
A token gibbet from which hung my effigy...
— O Lord! give me the strength and the tenacity
To view my body and my soul without disgust!

CXVII. – LOVE AND THE SKULL

Tailpiece

Love is seated on the skull
Of Humanity;
Thus enthroned, this heathen, full
Of effrontery

Blows round bubbles that unfurl
And ascend apace,
As if seeking other worlds
In the depths of space.

This translucent fragile sphere
Takes its rapid flight
Bursts and spits its contents clear
Out into the night.

When each bubble bursts, the skull
Trembles, and entreats:
— "This mad game is pitiful,
When is it to cease?

For what your foul bubbles rain
Down in copious flood,
Vile assassin, is my brain,
My flesh and my blood!"

REVOLT

CXVIII. – SAINT PETER'S DENIAL

What then does God do with this flood of blasphemies
That rises daily to his Seraphim divine?
Like any tyrant who has gorged on meat and wine,
He falls asleep, lulled by our vile profanities.

The sobs of martyrs and the cries of tortured men
Are doubtless an intoxicating symphony,
Because, though for their sins they have paid heavily,
The heavens have by no means had their fill of them!

— Jesus, think of the Garden of Gethsemane!
When you knelt down to pray, in all simplicity,
To him who in his heaven mocked your misery
When into your live flesh the nails sank painfully,

When you heard men deriding your divinity,
Blackguards and ruffians who wished to see you dead,
And when you felt the thorns sink deep into your head,
In which there dwelt the whole of our Humanity;

When the weight of your broken body, once so proud,
Stretched your extended arms, and when your sweat and
blood
Flowed from your livid brow in an incessant flood,
When you were raised in martyrdom before the crowd,

Did you dream of those glorious days and wondrous
hours
When you came to fulfil the covenant of God,
When, seated on an ass, in majesty you trod
The streets bestrewn with palms and garlanded with
flowers,

When, buoyed by faith and hope, devoid of doubt or fear,
You castigated money-lenders with such force,

In other words, when you were master? Did remorse
Not pierce your side far deeper than the soldier's spear?

— For my part, I shall leave this world well satisfied,
This world where dream and action dwell in disaccord;
Let me live by the sword and perish by the sword!
Saint Peter denied Christ... and he was justified!

CXIX. – ABEL AND CAIN

I

Tribe of Abel, eat, drink and sleep;
God smiles on you indulgently.

Tribe of Cain, slither and creep
Through the mire; die miserably.

Tribe of Abel, your sacrifice
Is pleasing to the Seraphim!

Tribe of Cain, when will the price
That you must pay satisfy Him?

Tribe of Abel, your flocks thrive
And your healthy crops abound;

Tribe of Cain, to stay alive
You eat the scraps that you have found.

Tribe of Abel, take your ease
At the patriarchal fire;

Tribe of Cain, tremble and freeze
Like a jackal in the mire!

Tribe of Abel, love, increase!
Gold brings forth new progeny.

Tribe of Cain, take heed and cease
Your appetite for cruelty.

Abel's tribe, you feed and grow
Like insects boring endlessly!

Tribe of Cain, your people go
In fear and insecurity.

II

Tribe of Abel, your remains
Will fertilise the steaming soil!

Tribe of Cain, it still remains
For you to profit from your toil;

Tribe of Abel, to your shame
The plough is vanquished by the sword!

Tribe of Cain, now stake your claim
To heaven, and cast out the Lord!

CXX. – THE LITANIES OF SATAN

O fairest of all Angels, wise in all your ways,
Spirit betrayed by destiny, deprived of praise,

Satan, have mercy on me in my misery!

O Prince of exile who from men have suffered wrong
And who, vanquished, always stand up again more
strong,

Satan, have mercy on me in my misery!

O great all-knowing king of subterranean things,
Familiar healer of all human sufferings,

Satan, have mercy on me in my misery!

You who give lepers and all those whom men despise,
Through your eternal love, a taste of Paradise,

Satan, have mercy on me in my misery!

You who, even from Death, your old and trusted mate,
Knew how to fashion Hope, - that charming opiate!

Satan, have mercy on me in my misery!

You who lend the doomed man a bearing calm and proud
Upon the scaffold, bringing shame upon the crowd.

Satan, have mercy on me in my misery!

You who know in what corners of this envious earth
A jealous God secreted gemstones of great worth,

Satan, have mercy on me in my misery!

You whose clear eye can see the arsenals and stores
Where lie, in slumber deep, great tribes of precious ores,

Satan, have mercy on me in my misery!

You whose broad hand conceals the fatal precipice
From the sleep-walker lost atop an edifice,

Satan, have mercy on me in my misery!

You who know how to render supple ageing bones
Of drunks trampled by horses on the cobblestones,

Satan, have mercy on me in my misery!

You who, to comfort frail and suffering humankind,
Taught us how sulphur and saltpetre are combined,

Satan, have mercy on me in my misery!

You who inscribe your mark, O comrade full of guile,
On the brow of a Croesus, pitiless and vile,

Satan, have mercy on me in my misery!

You who, upon the eyes and hearts of kindly whores,
Bestowed a love of ragged clothes and bleeding sores,

Satan, have mercy on me in my misery!

Staff of the exiled, guiding lamp of pioneers,
Confessor of condemned men and conspirators,

Satan, have mercy on me in my misery!

Adoptive father of all those whom in his wrath
The Lord God banished from his paradise on earth,

Satan, have mercy on me in my misery!

Prayer

All praise and glory, Satan, be to you on high,
In Heaven where you reigned, and in Hell where you lie
Defeated, dreaming silently. Grant that I may
Repose my weary soul beside your own one day,
Beneath the Tree of Knowledge whose branches shall
spread
Like a resurgent Temple over your proud head!

DEATH

CXXI. – THE DEATH OF LOVERS

We shall have beds imbued with subtle scents,
And ottomans as deep as any tomb,
And shelves with flowers strange and redolent,
That under fairer skies for us will bloom.

Burning ever more ardent and more bright,
Our hearts will shine like beacons from above,
Each sending forth their pure reflected light
To the twin mirrors of our endless love.

One evening made of rose and mystic blue,
We shall exchange an ultimate adieu,
A last scintilla of this earthly life;

And later an Angelic form will pass,
To faithfully and joyously revive
The dormant embers and the tarnished glass.

CXXII. – THE DEATH OF THE POOR

It's Death that comforts us, alas! and makes us live;
It is our lifetime's aim, our only hope and friend;
It fills us like an elixir, and seems to give
Us strength to tread the path of life until the end;

As we traverse the storms, the winters bleak and cold,
Upon our dark horizon it's the radiant beam,
It is the famous inn of which the book once told,
Where we shall sit and eat, and sleep, and idly dream;

It is the Angel who gives us his sanctuary,
Who brings the gift of sleep and blissful reverie,
Who makes the bed in which the naked pauper lies;

It is God's glory, his abode, his outstretched hand,
It is the poor man's purse and his true fatherland,
It is the open portal to the unknown Skies!

CXXIII. – THE DEATH OF ARTISTS

How often must I shake my little bells, and deign
To kiss your lowly brow, pathetic travesty?
To pierce your bull's-eye, target full of mystery,
How many arrows must my quiver give in vain?

We shall consume our souls in many subtle schemes,
And we'll demolish many armatures before
We contemplate the great Creation we adore,
For which we yearn and weep in our most ardent dreams!

Those who have never known the Idol of their soul,
The sculptors who are damned and suffer obloquy,
Who go beating their breast and brow in misery,

Have but one hope, bizarre and sombre Capitol!
It is that Death, like a new sun above their tomb,
Will make the flowers of their spirit grow and bloom!

CXXIV. – THE END OF THE DAY

Beneath a pale, depressing light,
Twisting and dancing pointlessly
Goes Life, gaudy and uncontrite.
And so, when Night voluptuously

On the horizon speaks its name,
Assuaging hunger, healing past
Humiliation, even shame,
The Poet tells himself: "At last!

My spirit, like my vertebrae,
Ardently yearns for sweet release,
And rapt in sombre reverie

I shall lie down to take my ease,
Wrapped in the blanket of your peace,
O comforting obscurity!"

CXXV. – THE DREAM OF A CURIOUS MAN

To Félix Nadar

Do you perchance, like me, feel pleasurable dole,
And do they say of you: "This man's an oddity!"
— I was about to die, and in my fevered soul
Desire mingled with dread, a curious malady;

Anguish and hope, devoid of any factious whim.
The more the sands of time fatally gathered pace,
The more my pain became both comforting and grim;
My heart was being torn from its familiar place.

I was the child who longs to see the spectacle,
Hating the curtain as a needless obstacle...
Finally the cold truth revealed itself to me:

Death had brought no surprise, no agony or thrill -
Just the cold light of day. — What? Is that all we see?
The curtain had gone up, and I was waiting still.

CXXVI. – THE JOURNEY

To Maxime Du Camp

I

To children who delight in maps and colour plates,
The world is equal only to their appetite.
Bright lights can make it seem such an enormous place!
And yet how small it is, considered with hindsight!

One morning we depart, our hearts and minds afire,
Carried on waves that rise and fall rhythmically,
Filled with a gnawing rancour and bitter desire,
Cradling infinite thoughts upon the finite sea:

Some of us, glad to flee a country we despise,
Others, the horror of their birthplace, others still,
Astrologers immersed in a strange woman's eyes,
Subjected to the tyranny of perfumed Circe's will.

In order not to be transmuted into swine,
They drink their fill of light from realms of fiery space;
The icy winds that blow, the blazing suns that shine,
Slowly erase the marks left by her vile embrace.

But the true voyagers are those who put to sea
Simply for travel's sake; they press on, hearts aglow,
Never leaving the path of their true destiny
And, without knowing why, they always say: Let's go!

Those whose ardent desires resemble cumulus,
Who dream, like a recruit might dream about the gun,
Of pleasures ever-changing, vast, voluptuous,
Whose name has never been revealed to anyone!

II

We imitate, O horror! balls and spinning tops
That, even while we sleep, gyrate and bounce and run,
And Curiosity, cruel Angel, never stops
Tormenting us, like suns that she has whipped and spun.

Strange destiny whose goal is always on the move,
And, being nowhere, can be anywhere, who knows!
Where Man, whose steadfast hope no obstacle can move,
Continues his eternal quest to find repose!

Our soul is like a ship seeking Icaria;
"Look what's ahead!" a voice calls out in disbelief.
Another, from the mast, shouts in euphoria:
"O joy and happiness!" — Damnation! It's a reef!

Each tiny island that the lookout boy might see
Is taken to be Eldorado, our last dock;
Imagination, spreading out its panoply,
In the cold light of day finds nothing but a rock.

O that poor lover of exotic chimeras!
Should we clap him in irons and cast him to the sea,
That drunken sailor who sees new Americas
Whose mirage makes the oceans flow more bitterly?

So too the aged vagrant, trudging through the mud,
Dreaming, nose in the air, of castles shining bright;
His ever-spellbound eye sees a new Capua
In every humble dwelling lit by candlelight.

III

Amazing voyagers! What noble histories
We read within the depths of your enchanting eyes!
Show us the caskets of your fertile memories,
Those incandescent gems, garnered from stars and skies.

We too would cross the seas, but without sail or steam!
To lighten our ennui, where every day's the same,
Imbue our spirits with your memories and dreams,
Like a great canvas that the vast horizons frame.

Tell us, what have you seen?

IV

      "We have seen many stars
And many waves; we have seen many beaches too;
And despite many blows, of which we bear the scars,
We often felt the weight of boredom, just like you.

The glory of the sun's rays on the violet sea,
The glory of the spires that in the sunset rise,
Ignited in our hearts a strange anxiety
To savour the delights promised by azure skies.

But opulent cities, great pageantries, vast crowds,
Could never hold for us the mystical allure
Of those scenes which by chance are conjured in the
clouds.
And desire always left us anxious and unsure!

Enjoyment bolsters up and strengthens our desire.
Desire, old tree for whom delight is your manure,
Your bark grows thick and hard, and your branches grow
higher,
Striving to reach the sky, drawn by the sun's allure

Will you grow ever taller, great tree more robust
Than even the cypress? — But from our wanderings
We've saved some sketches for your album, you who must
Assuage your avid yearnings for exotic things!

We've bowed to graven images and effigies;
Fine thrones inset with gems of quality supreme;
Opulent palaces whose fabled luxuries
Would be for any banker a ruinous dream.

Costumes that are inebriation for the eyes;
Women with teeth and nails tinted with subtle stains,
And snake charmers whose skills astonish and surprise."

V

And then, and then what else?

VI

                   "O simple childlike brains!

We must never forget the most important thing:
Across the entire spectrum of humanity,
We witnessed, without seeking, in our wandering,
The tedious round of sin and immorality:

Woman, base slave, self-loving and contemptuous,
Yet unaware that she's so stupid and so vain;
And man, obsessed by greed, wanton, libidinous,
Slave of the slave and gutter flowing in the drain;

The torturer's delight, the martyr's agony;
The feast seasoned by blood to feed the despot's urge;
The lust for power and the curse of tyranny,
The crowd amorous of the brutalising scourge;

Many religions that are not unlike our own,
All aiming for the sky; and Saintly Piety,
Like a voluptuary upon his bed of down,
Seeking in nails and sackcloth its felicity;

Drunk on its genius, prattling Humanity
That's just as crazy now as it's been from the first,
Shouting to God, in its unbridled agony,
"O Master, my own likeness, may you now be cursed!"

And those less stupid, brave friends of Insanity,
Fleeing the servile flock that Fate has herded in,
And seeking refuge in opium's sanctuary!
— Such is the entire globe's eternal bulletin."

VII

Such bitter knowledge that we all draw from our voyage!
The world, monotonous and petty, lets us see,
Today, yesterday and tomorrow, our own image:
An oasis of horror in a desert of ennui!

Should we depart? or stay? If you can't stay, then go;
Stay if you can. One runs, another secretly
Remains to thwart harsh Time, that unrelenting foe!
There are, alas! those who are running constantly,

Like the apostles or the lonely wandering Jew,
To whom nothing avails, neither carriage nor ship,
To flee this vicious combatant; there are a few
Who know how to slay him without leaving their crib.

When finally he catches up with us, at least
We shall still foster hope, and shout aloud: Let's go!
Just as in former times we set off for the East,
Eyes fixed on the horizon, and with cheeks aglow

We shall embark upon the Sea of Darkness, where
We'll sail, like a young passenger, in joyful haste.
Do you hear those alluring, deathlike voices there,
That sing: "This way please, those of you who wish to taste

The perfumed Lotus! This is where we gather in
The wondrous fruits whose flavour every joy transcends.
Come and taste their delights, forever savouring
The magic of an afternoon that never ends!"

In those familiar tones we recognise the spectre;
Our friends, like Pylades, stretch out their arms to us.
"To replenish your heart swim out to your Electra!"
Says she whose knees in former times we used to kiss.

VIII

O Death, old captain, let's cast off! The time has come!
This country holds no joy for us. Come! Let's depart!
Although both sky and sea are bathed in inky gloom,
You know that your bright flame still burns in every heart!

Pour us your poisoned draught, and let its comfort dwell
Within us; let your ardent fire our hearts imbue;
We'll fathom the abyss, be it Heaven or Hell,
To seek out the Unknown, and to find something *new*!

THE BANNED POEMS

I. – LESBOS

Mother of Latin games and Greek voluptuousness,
Lesbos, where long caresses bring such sweet delights,
Some full of ardent passion, some full of tenderness,
To glorious summer days and sultry wanton nights.
Mother of Latin games and Greek voluptuousness,

Lesbos, where love's caresses flow like cataracts,
Cascading fearlessly into the deep abyss,
Rebounding, sobbing, laughing, making secret pacts,
Delighting in the storms engendered by each kiss.
Lesbos, where love's caresses flow like cataracts!

Lesbos, where every Phryne has her concubine,
Where never did a sigh remain without echo,
You equal starlit Paphos in your grace divine,
And Venus might justly be envious of Sappho!
Lesbos, where every Phryne has her concubine,

Lesbos, exotic land of sultry, languid nights,
Where, in their looking-glass, O sterile wantonness!
Young girls with hollow eyes, in love with their delights,
Bestow upon their nubile charms a soft caress;
Lesbos, exotic land of sultry, languid nights,

Let old austere Plato knit his brow in a frown;
Your pardon can be found in kisses and caresses,
Queen of this noble land, isle of peerless renown,
And in refinements that know nothing of excesses.
Let old austere Plato knit his brow in a frown.

Your pardon can be found in the eternal pain
Suffered by hearts in which too much ambition lies,
Lured, by a radiant smile, from their secure domain,
That beckons from the confines of more distant skies!
Your pardon can be found in the eternal pain!

Which of the Gods, Lesbos, will dare to be your judge,
Condemning your pale brow, that has toiled ceaselessly,
Before his golden scales have weighed the heavy flood
Of tears which your torrents have poured into the sea?
Which of the Gods, Lesbos, will dare to be your judge?

What care we for the laws of what's just and unjust?
Maidens of whose renown these islands proudly tell,
Your faith, as any faith, is noble and august,
And love can laugh at Heaven as it can laugh at Hell!
What care we for the laws of what's just or unjust?

For Lesbos chose me from all poets on the earth,
To praise the flowering virgins that this isle reveres,
For I have known the mystery, almost from birth,
Of their unbridled laughter and their sombre tears;
For Lesbos chose me from all poets on the earth.

Since then I have kept watch from the Leucadian height,
Like a lone sentry with a sure and piercing gaze
For frigates, trawlers, sailboats heaving into sight,
Whose distant silhouettes fluctuate in the haze.
Since then I have kept watch from the Leucadian height,

To see whether the sea is good and bountiful,
If in the sobbing of its waves it is kind-hearted,
And will give back to Lesbos, who is merciful,
The venerated corpse of Sappho, who departed
To see whether the sea is good and bountiful!

Of masculine Sappho, lover and poetess,
Fairer than Venus in her pale melancholy!
— The azure eye is vanquished by the dolefulness
Of the dark ring traced by the pain and misery
Of masculine Sappho, lover and poetess!

— Fairer than Venus towering above the world
And pouring forth her charms by which men are beguiled,
With the effulgence of her youthful locks unfurled
Upon the old Ocean, enchanted by his child;
Fairer than Venus towering above the world!

— Of Sappho who succumbed to blasphemy that day,
When, scornful of the cult to which she owed fealty,
She wantonly allowed her body to fall prey
To a proud brute who punished the impiety
Of Sappho who succumbed to blasphemy that day.

And since that fatal day proud Lesbos must lament
And, although honoured by a world that she adores,
Be haunted every night by cries of great torment
That rise towards the sky from her deserted shores.
And since that fatal day proud Lesbos must lament!

II. – DAMNED WOMEN (Delphine and Hippolyta)

In the pale light of lamps that flickered languidly,
On lavish cushions that were redolent with scents
Hippolyta recalled, in silent reverie,
The kisses that had stolen her young innocence.

She sought, her troubled gaze blurred by the storm, the
skies
Of her virginity, already far away,
As might a voyager who vainly turns his eyes
Toward the blue horizons passed earlier in the day.

The idle tears that filled her dull eyes, once so bright,
The broken look, the stupor, the weary wantonness,
Her arms, like useless weapons cast aside in flight,
All serving to adorn her fragile comeliness.

Languidly at her feet, Delphine contented lay,
Ardently watching her, eyes blazing with delight,
Like a strong, savage beast that gazes on its prey,
On which its teeth have left the imprint of its bite.

Strong beauty proudly kneeling at frail beauty's feet,
Savouring the bouquet, voluptuous and lewd,
Of her triumphant wine, and in her vain conceit
Soliciting a token of sweet gratitude.

Expectantly she sought in her pale victim's eye
The silent canticle that purest pleasure sings,
And the infinite gratitude that, like a sigh,
Escapes in subtle glances from mysterious springs.

— Hippolyta, dear heart, what say you of these things?
Do you now understand you must not sacrifice
The sacred holocaust of your first flowerings
To harsh caresses that exact a heavy price?

My kisses are as gentle as the mayfly's wings
That silently caress the surface of the lake,
While those of a male lover wreak destructive things,
Like the deep grooves that chariots' wheels and
ploughshares make.

They'll trample over you, like a lumbering team
Of horses and of oxen, their hooves with iron shod...
Hippolyta, my sister! My sweet enduring dream,
My spirit and my soul, my wondrous gift from God,

Turn unto me your eyes of starlight and azure!
For one beguiling glance, divine balm, radiant beam,
I shall unveil a store of pleasures more obscure,
And lull you gently in a never-ending dream!"

Then said Hippolyta, raising her youthful head:
— "It's not ingratitude or remorse that I feel,
My Delphine, yet I suffer and am filled with dread
After this dark and terrible nocturnal meal.

I feel a heavy torment hanging over me,
With dark battalions of sparse demonic shapes
Leading me down strange pathways of uncertainty,
Hemmed in by horizons from which there's no escape.

Have we therefore engaged in an illicit pleasure?
Tell me, why do I feel such sorrow and such fear?
I tremble when I hear you say to me: 'My treasure!'
And yet my lips are drawn to yours when you are near.

Do not look at me thus, my dearest sister whom
I shall forever hold in deepest adoration,
Even were you to be a snare set for my doom
And the beginning of my eternal damnation!"

Delphine arose and proudly shook her tragic mane,
And wildly seeking what the tripod might foretell,
With fatal eye, responded in despotic vein:
— "Who in love's presence dares to speak the name of
hell?

May he be ever cursed who fostered useless dreams,
Who was the first to try, in his stupidity,
To fashion sterile edicts and misguided schemes
That mingle things erotic with integrity!

He who would merge into a mystical accord
Shadows with light and warmth, and daytime with the
night,
Will never warm himself nor garner a reward
Beneath this radiant sun of amorous delight.

Go, if you wish, and seek a stupid paramour;
Offer your virgin heart to his cruel caress;
And, filled with dire remorse, repentance and dolour,
You will bring back to me your violated breasts...

Woman here on this earth can only serve one master!"
But the sweet child, by anxious torment torn apart,
Suddenly cried: - "I feel, opening ever faster,
A yawning chasm; and that chasm is my heart!!

Neither the depths of hell, nor the volcano's rage
Will ever satisfy this groaning monster's ire!
And nothing can the Fury's dreadful thirst assuage,
Who, flaming torch in hand, consumes its blood with fire.

Let our drawn curtains set us from the world apart,
And may our lassitude bring us eternal rest!
I want to sleep forever in your beating heart,
And feel the coolness of the tomb upon your breast!"

— Descend, descend, pitiful victims, it is time
To fathom the abyss of hell's eternal fire!
Plunge into its vast depths where every human crime,
Whipped by a wind too fierce even for heaven's ire,

Bubbles and effervesces in a storm-like rage.
Mad shadows, your desires will not be compromised;
Never will you be able your passions to assuage,
And by your very pleasures you will be chastised.

No ray of light shall penetrate your dismal lair;
Only feverish miasma passing through small vents,
Dimly illumining the dark and fetid air,
And infusing your bodies with their lurid scents.

The harsh sterility of your lasciviousness
Quickens your raging thirst and vitrifies your skin,
And the unbridled wind of your licentiousness
Causes your flesh to flap in penance for its sin.

In exile from this world, you must your path pursue
Through wild and barren lands, wandering aimlessly,
Fleeing the infinite that still resides in you,
Poor disconnected souls, to find your destiny!

III. – THE LETHE

Unyielding soul, come to my heart once more,
Beloved tigress with the languid air;
I want to run my fingers through your hair,
Those heavy golden tresses I adore.

Within your skirts, filled with your scent, to hide
My aching head as in a secret bower,
And breathe once more, as from a withered flower,
The tainted fragrance of a love that died.

I want to sleep, rather than live, alas!
In slumber that is bittersweet as death,
Spreading my shameless kisses and my breath
Upon your body smooth as polished brass.

To drown my muted sobs there's no abyss
That equals the deep haven of your breast;
Your lips speak of oblivion's sweet rest,
And silent Lethe courses in your kiss.

To my destiny, henceforth my delight,
My staunch obedience is preordained;
A docile martyr who's unjustly blamed,
Whose fervour serves to amplify his plight,

I'll suck, to drown my rancour's aching smart,
Nepenthe and the hemlock's bitter zest
From the sweet promontories of this breast
That never gave asylum to a heart.

IV. – TO HER WHO IS TOO GAY

Your head, your bearing and your grace
Are like a charming landscape, where,
Like zephyr breezes in the air,
Sweet laughter plays upon your face.

Sad souls you pass along the way
Are dazzled by the radiant health
That shines in such abundant wealth
From your sublime décolleté.

Resplendent colours that enhance
The beauty of your fine array
Inspire upon the poet's eye
The image of a floral dance.

These mad creations symbolise
The multi-coloured spirit of
A woman whom I madly love,
And also hate, in equal wise.

Oft, in a garden seeking rest,
I dragged my sluggish atony,
And felt, O bitter irony!
The sunlight tearing at my breast,

And springtime's green magnificence
Cast such despair upon my heart
That on a flower I did impart
Revenge for Nature's insolence.

And in the night-time, secretly,
When tolls the bell of volupty,
Into your carnal treasury
I'll creep, a coward, silently,

There to chastise your comely flesh,
To bruise your now forgiven breast,
And carve on your astonished side
A wound so cavernous and wide,

And — heady sweetness that enthrals!
— Into those fresh lips' gaping walls
Where new joys and delights appear,
I'll spurt my venom, sister dear!

V. – THE JEWELS

My dearest love was naked, and, knowing my heart,
Retained as sole attire her most sonorous gems,
Whose opulent display resembled the proud art
Of Moorish concubines bedecked with diadems.

When, shaken, it emits a lively mocking sound,
This radiant world of metal and resplendent stones
Fills me with ecstasy, for I have always found
Joy in the subtle interplay of light and tones.

And there she lay in languorous cupidity,
Smiling as she looked down upon her willing slave,
Upon my love, as deep as the eternal sea,
That flowed towards her being, as to the cliffs the wave.

Like a tame tiger, gazing at me fixedly,
She dreamily adopted miscellaneous poses,
Combining artlessness with impropriety,
Which lent a novel charm to her metamorphoses;

And her arms and her legs, and her loins and her thighs,
Undulating, swanlike, with softly silken shine,
Serenely passed before my penetrating eyes;
And her belly and breasts, those sweet grapes of my vine,

Advanced, like wanton Angels, in their sweet allure,
Disturbing the repose in which my soul had been,
And shattering the rock of crystal clear and pure
On which she had reposed, solitary and serene.

I thought I saw united in a new design
Antiope's ample hips with the bust of a boy,
The slimness of her waist lending her pelvic shrine
More prominence; and its dark colouring, what joy!

— As the bedchamber's lamplight was resigned to die,
Only the glowing hearth lit up the space therein;
And every time it uttered a flamboyant sigh,
It emblazoned with blood her amber-coloured skin!

VI. – THE METAMORPHOSES OF THE VAMPIRE

The woman meanwhile made her body writhe and roll
Like a snake on an incandescent bed of coal;
She pressed her breasts into the metal of her busk,
And from her ruby lips came words laden with musk:
— "Behold, my lips are moist, and I have learnt the art
Of swooning to the joys seduction can impart.
I dry everyone's tears on my triumphant breasts,
And I make old men laugh as children laugh at jests.
Divested of attire, my naked form will vie
With the sun and the moon, and the stars and the sky!
I am, my learned friend, so versed in wanton charms,
That when I hold a mortal in my fearsome arms,
Or when I offer up to avid bites my bust,
Timid and libertine, and fragile and robust,
Upon these mattresses that swoon in ecstasy,
Debilitated angels would damn themselves for me!"

But when she had sucked all the marrow out of me,
And when again I turned towards her languidly
To render her a loving kiss, I could see just
A viscous, oozing wineskin, full of fetid pus!
I closed my eyes in horror at this ghastly sight,
And when I opened them again, in the harsh light,
Instead of that proud woman, lying by my side,
Whose vampire lust I thought my blood had satisfied,
There trembled in confusion a skeleton's remains,
From which came a loud rattle, like a weathervane
Or a shop sign suspended from an iron spike,
Buffeted by the wind on a wild winter's night.

OTHER POEMS

I. — SELF-COMMUNION

Be gentle, O my Sorrow; come now, settle down;
The evening shadows you so longed for now appear;
A veil of darkness has descended on the town,
To some affording peace, to others doubt and fear.

While the vile multitude its recreation seeks
Beneath the cruel scourge of Pleasure's tyranny,
Gathering sore contrition in the servile feast,
My Sorrow, take my hand, and come away with me,

Far from them. See the bygone Years their vigil keep,
On heaven's balconies, in antiquated dress,
While simpering Regret emerges from the deep.

The dying Sun's last embers sink beneath an arch,
And, like an endless shroud trailing towards the East,
Hear, my beloved, hear Night's gentle onward march.

II. — TO MR EUGÈNE FROMENTIN (CONCERNING A BORE WHO CONSIDERED HIMSELF A FRIEND)

He told me he was very rich,
But that he feared the cholera;
— That he was careful with his cash
But that he loved the opera;

— That Nature left him much inspired,
Being by Corot ably taught;
— And although not as yet acquired,
A carriage would be shortly bought;

— That he loved marble, slate and brick,
And golden wood of finest grade;
— That in his workshop he possessed
Three craftsmen masters of their trade;

— That he had, not to count the rest,
Twenty thousand shares in the North;
— And that he'd purchased, for a song,
Some picture frames by Oppenord;

— That he'd go even to Luzarches
To find the best of bric-à-brac,
And from the mart of Patriarches
He'd always bring some treasures back;

— That he did not much like his wife
Nor his dear mother, sad to say,
And yet he sought eternal life,
And knew the works of Niboyet!

— That he'd a taste for carnal love,
And on a tedious Roman stay
A woman, stricken by phthisis,
Of love for him had passed away.

For fully three hours and a half
This chatterbox, come from Tournai,
Churned out the story of his life –
I thought my brain would burst that day!

If I tried to describe my pain,
I'd never know quite when to cease;
And hoping not to go insane,
I thought: "Dear God, give me some peace!"

And like one who is ill at ease,
But cannot make good his escape,
I rubbed my bottom on my seat
And dreamt of his impending fate.

That monster, Bastogne is his name,
Was fleeing from the dreaded plague;
I'd flee as far as Gascony,
Or throw myself into the Seine,

If, in this Paris he so fears,
When we have all returned some day,
My path should ever cross again
That tiresome dullard from Tournai.

III. — TO THÉODORE DE BANVILLE

So firmly did you grasp the Goddess by her hair
That, judging by your mastery and nonchalance,
You might have been compared, forgive my impudence,
To some young ruffian flooring his mistress there.

With clarity of eye, with such precocity,
You've shown how proud you are to be an architect
Of writings which are so audaciously correct
That in them we foresee your full maturity.

Poet, our blood escapes through every single pore;
Was it merely by chance the robe of the Centaur,
Which to a morbid stream transmuted every vein,

Was three times dipped and tinted by the subtle biles
Of these monstrous, vindictive, hideous reptiles
That in his crib the infant Heracles had slain?

Index of titles and first lines

Printed in Great Britain
by Amazon.co.uk, Ltd.,
Marston Gate.